MY NECK OF TH

C000172779

MY NECK OF THE WOODS

A Childhood in Bedford's Black Tom

Violet Tompkins

WHISTLING PUBLISHERS

First published in 2006 by
Whistling Publishers
285 Bedford Road, Rushden, Northamptonshire NN10 0SQ

Copyright © Violet Groocock 2006
All rights reserved

ISBN 0-9553844-0-0
ISBN 978-0-9553844-0-0

Design and production by Peter Flower Design

Printed in Great Britain by
Woolnough Bookbinding Ltd

Acknowledgements

I would like thank Richard Wildman for his encouragement; my daughter Sarah for her help with editing; Peter Flower for his technical expertise; Bedfordshire Archives and Record Service; Bedford Central Library; and Mrs Joyce (Irving) Ingle, Mrs Janet (Daniel) Allen, Mrs Joan (Humphreys) Darlow, the late Mr Feneley and Mr Terry Darlow for the loan of photographs.

For my dad

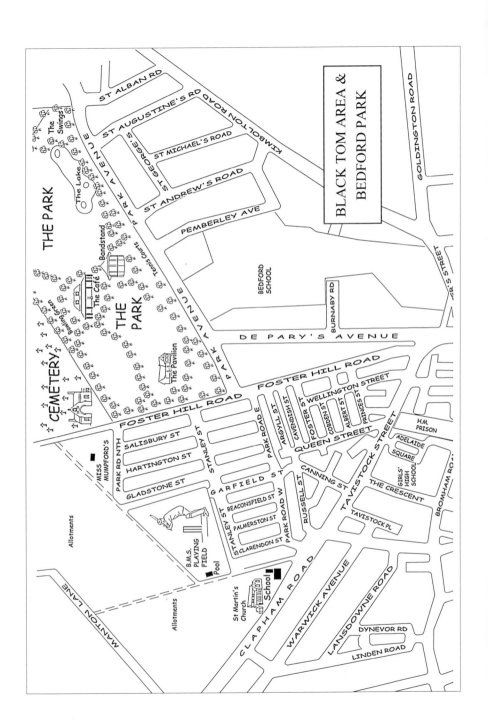

Contents

CHAPTER 1   From the Cradle to the Grave   11

CHAPTER 2   Playtime   31

CHAPTER 3   School Days   57

CHAPTER 4   Wartime   83

CHAPTER 5   After the War   105

Additional Photographs   117

Jim Tompkins in Salisbury Street 1950.

1

FROM THE CRADLE TO THE GRAVE

I was born and bred in the Black Tom area of Bedford, which is said to have been named after a highwayman who was hanged at the junction of Union Street, Tavistock Street and Clapham Road. My Great Granny Tompkins, who died in 1952 at the age of 97, said it was named after an African called Black Tom who was murdered in Cut Throat Lane, off Clapham Road (near the west spur of the Clapham Bypass roundabout).

It was certainly *not* named after the three black-faced coal merchants who lived and traded in Black Tom. The youngest (and always the blackest) of these was my father, Jim Tompkins of 79 Garfield Street. He had a coal yard at the house, and when he bagged up coal, the dust settling on his sweating face made him very black. His bright white teeth gleamed from his happy black face, and he was many a housewife's favourite. As he did his rounds they provided him with cups of tea and home-made cakes. One of these women, when paying for her coal, actually said to my mother, 'If anything happens to you, I'd willingly take your Jim on!'

Most of his customers lived in north Bedford, and he was

well known with his horse and coal cart. Dad never hawked his coal (all of it was previously ordered), but he would serve occasional customers who came to the house, often at ungodly hours, with a half-hundredweight of coal. He was always a soft touch and often didn't get paid. He never became a wealthy man.

Half way down Garfield Street was another coal merchant, Cecil Daniel. 'Dan', as Dad always called him, delivered coal with a lorry as most of his customers lived further away. During the Second World War, his lorry was requisitioned by the Government and he had to use a horse and cart. Dan knew very little about horses, and he needed to learn quickly, so it was to my dad that he turned and from then on they became very good friends.

The third coal merchant was Jack Fowler, who lived just round the corner in Park Road East (now called Roff Avenue). Whenever Jack delivered coal to a public house, his horse was usually rewarded with a pint of beer. It regularly drank at the Balloon in Foster Hill Road, and on one occasion was photographed for the local paper. I believe it also drank at the Fox in Park Road West. When Jack Fowler went into hospital for an operation, my dad sometimes used Jack's horse (instead of his own) to keep it exercised. Unfortunately for my dad, the horse would not walk past these pubs and would stop for a pint. It didn't get one with my dad on the end of the reins, and the animal had to be gently cajoled to move on.

I was my parents' only child and born at the Garfield Street family home on 5th February, 1932. The house belonged at that time to my great-grandparents, Loammi and

Cecil Daniel with one of his lorries.

My father, Jim Tompkins, outside the stable with the horse. The hole in the hay loft door was to let the cats in. They kept the mice away.

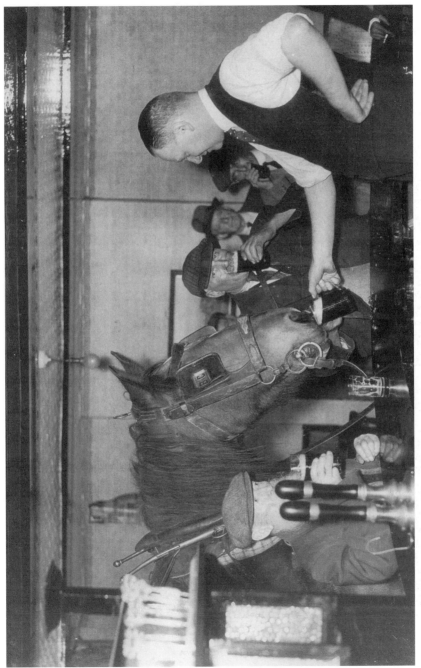

Reg Humphreys offers Jack Fowler's horse a pint at the Balloon public house in Foster Hill Road.

Loammi Tompkins and family outside 79 Garfield Street in the early 1900s. From left: daughter Emily, his mother Mahalah Odell, Loammi and daughter Cissie.

Elizabeth Tompkins. They had come to Bedford from Stagsden, and lived at 43 Canning Street until our house was built, at the top end of Garfield Street, in the late 1870s. It was an ugly house – built by, and to the taste of, Granddad's mother, Mahalah Odell, who lived with them until she died in 1913. It had adjoining stables, a hay loft and cart sheds. (The house has now been converted into two flats, and a new house and offices built in the yard.) It was the first building to be constructed in Garfield or Stanley Street, and Granny Odell used the surrounding open land to keep chickens and a goat – which she regularly 'set on' cheeky or unruly boys. She had the reputation of being a bit of a tyrant, if not a witch!

Granddad was a very good horse doctor. After the First World War, he took on blinded and shell-shocked horses which had come back from the front. He gradually turned them into working animals again. During the Second World War, we had the vet to look at one of our horses. The first thing he said to my dad was, 'The old feller's dead then, or you'd never have called me out!' The vet had sometimes been called if our pigs had erysipelas, but he had never before been needed for a sick horse.

Granddad had started a coal business in the 1880s, but it had virtually run down by the time my father started his rounds in 1920, at the age of fourteen. Many of Granddad's customers lived in the villages surrounding Bedford, and he delivered coal to a number of village pubs. Unfortunately, the publicans often paid for their fuel in kind. When Granddad was drunk, they would put him on the coal cart, smack the horse's rump, and the horse would bring him safely home.

Consequently, on principle, my dad would never serve a public house; but when the Second World War broke out and coal was rationed, the Kent in Salisbury Street registered with him.

When Garfield Street was completely built up, its shops and trades could service us almost from the cradle to the grave. The midwife, Nurse Barker, lived round the corner in Beaconsfield Street; while the undertaker, Mr Archie Street, lived and worked at number 49 Garfield Street. He was also a carpenter and joiner.

Day Brothers were butchers who had their shop and slaughterhouse on the corner with Park Road West. They made deliveries with an old-fashioned, three-wheeled van of the type elaborately decorated and still used in some Mediterranean countries.

Mrs Prior had a shop at number 48 Garfield Street which must have sold groceries; but I can only remember the sweets, sherbet dabs and the lucky bags with a 'diamond ring' to fasten the top. The sweets displayed in the window, next to the glass, had been there for so long they had gone rotten. (This shop was later bought by the Co-op.)

Next was Cecil Daniel, the coal merchant, who had a yard where he kept his lorry but did not stock coal. His hobby was breeding Dutch rabbits, which he entered in shows and for which he won prizes.

If you wanted to place a bet, there was a bookmaker at number 62.

At one time Miss French ran a sweet shop from the front room of her immaculately-kept house at number 64. She sold such novelties as imitation cigarettes, liquorice pipes and 'shoelaces' – you tore the 'laces' from a length of indented, inch-wide liquorice which was rolled into a coil with a sweet, covered in hundreds and thousands, in the middle.

On the corner of Stanley Street and the cul-de-sac of Garfield Street was a haberdasher's and clothes shop. In its windows, facing onto both streets, were mannequins of children dressed in school clothes. The rest of the window area was crammed with stiff collars, socks, underclothes and any small article you might need to wear. It was owned by my dad's uncle, E. J. Tompkins, until the mid 1930s. Afterwards, for a short time, Mr Cooper used it as a sweet shop and ran a Christmas club for sweets and chocolate. It was eventually taken over by the Misses Payne, who sold toiletries, stockings, ribbons, cottons, embroidery silks and the like.

This cul-de-sac was my end of the street. There were three houses on each side and it ended with a small wall, topped with a high iron railing, behind which was the Bedford Modern School playing field. There was a matching gate in the middle of the railings which was always kept locked, but boys used to climb over it. Old Mr Johnson at number 83, the last house, did his best to stop them by brandishing his walking stick. Mr Johnson's hobby was breeding budgerigars, which he kept in an aviary at the bottom of his garden. His wife had a dear little West Highland terrier. The old man spent a good deal of time at the corner of the street, leaning against our tall brick gatepost, watching the world go by. Children were very wary of him because as they walked past, just for fun (or so he thought) he might collar them by the neck with the crook of his stick.

At our house on the corner we kept three horses in the stables; in one of the cart sheds we kept rabbits in hutches; cats had their kittens in the hay loft, and chickens roamed the yard. One cockerel took a dislike to certain people and would attack them with both its feet. My Grandma Hills said it only attacked people who it sensed were afraid of it. She changed her mind the day it flew onto her shoulder and attacked her best hat with its beak. That Christmas it was 'on the table' – the bird, not the hat!

We also kept a pig bin in the yard where neighbours deposited their potato peelings, scraps of food and often, by mistake, their vegetable knives – the windowsill by the back door displayed these for collection. The swill was boiled and mixed with bran before it was fed to Dad's pigs on his Hoo Farm smallholding.

On the opposite corner of Stanley Street and Garfield Street was a grocer's, which, over the years, was owned by various shopkeepers. The first I can remember was Mrs Knowles, who sold all the usual provisions including sterilized milk, which came in bottles with a resealable, wire-sprung cap. Later owners included Mr Greenstead, Charles Hewitt and Mr Howard. Eventually Mr Rehberger used it as a printer and stationer's shop.

At one time we had two tailors in Garfield Street. Mr French, at number 67, displayed on the wall by his front door a small marble slab showing his name and trade. Next to him, at number 65, lived Mr Jones, who was a tailor by profession, I believe, but who also kept a shop and off-licence at number

63. Between his house and the shop front was a pair of double doors with a paved ramp for rolling barrels in and out of the off-licence. As small children we enjoyed playing on this ramp, using it to see whose marble, ball or wheeled toy would reach the bottom first. Another joy for us kids was that this shop had two entrances: one in Garfield Street, and another, by way of a long open passage, in Gladstone Street. It was great fun, when playing hide and seek, to go in one door, ask for something you knew they hadn't got (like chocolate before sweet ration coupons were issued) and go out of the other.

The off-licence also sold patent medicines and was used as our out-of-hours pharmacy. For a headache, you could buy a paper strip of Aspros; a tin of Zubes lozenges to ease a sore throat; or a small bottle of olive oil to relieve earache. Numerous varieties of bottles of cough cure, little boxes of Carnation Corn Ointment, plasters, and Beecham's Pills 'worth a guinea a box' were secured by elastic loops on cards advertising their benefits. Eyebrows would be raised at the purchase of a box of Beecham's rather than the paper twist of only three pills.

Mr Ives ran the shop during most of the Second World War and for some years after. It was he who put a stop to our in-one-door-and-out-of-the-other games and made sure that we came in and went out by the same door. Returning beer bottles, at a penny a time, was a good source of pocket money, until Mr Ives insisted on accepting only bottles which had been bought from his shop. It put a stop to my efforts at making money because my dad never bought bottled beer, so Mr Ives knew that any bottles I brought back had come from somewhere else. It was more than likely that Mr Ives had secretly marked the labels on his bottles. Later the shop was run by Mr Valentine; but whoever was the proprietor, the shop was always referred to as 'Joneses'.

At numbers 57–59, Leslie Banks had a bakery and shop. Bread rolls have never tasted as good as those bought hot from his ovens. He also ran a bakery round in the villages.

The street had two builders: Mr Jessop at number 55, and Corby's at number 74, although Corby's builder's yard was in Tavistock Street, near the Flower Pot pub. The Corby daughters were athletic and accomplished sportswomen.

In 'Little' Garfield Street, south of Park Road East, at number 9, Mrs Peplow kept a corn merchant's shop. From large wooden feed bins she sold pigeon corn, wheat, bran and crushed oats, which she shovelled up with a metal scoop and weighed in a large, coal-scuttle-shaped pan on an Avery scale. There were biscuits and Bob Martin's powders for dogs, Carswood Poultry Spice for mixing in with chicken feed to make hens lay better, and a selection of grits (oyster shell was the best) to improve the egg shells. She sold packets and bottles of patent medicines for all types of animals. During the war there were long queues for raw dog meat, which came from the knackers – whose job it was to slaughter old and sick horses and farm animals and who were licensed to sell the meat to pet shops. The meat was dyed purple (the dye was referred to as 'kybosh') to stop people eating it. I was recently told by a knacker's man that it could be, and often was, doctored by unscrupulous traders and used for human consumption, but I never heard of anyone who actually sold it for food, or anyone who knowingly ate it.

At number 7, Jock Small took over Mr Bruce's modern shoe-mending shop. The shining but noisy machinery he used to do the job was fascinating, and very different from that of the 'snob' (or cobbler) Jimmy Jones who traded within spitting distance in Queen Street. Jimmy Jones sat on a stool in his front room and cobbled shoes on a last held between his knees.

On the corner of Garfield Street, at number 68 Russell Street, was, in the 1930s, a milliner's or hat shop. Next door, at number 70, was Palphrey's barber's shop. When children went to have their hair done they were seated on a board placed across the arms of a wooden chair. My mother sent me there to get my hair cut: short, straight and with a fringe. She always grumbled at the result, but never complained to the barber and sent me there time and time again. Next to the barber's was Whittemore's Greengrocers, which later became Whittemore's Electrical Engineers.

Irving's the tobacconist and newsagent was at number 74 Russell Street. For six years I did a paper round for them. We had to sort out the papers and magazines at the back of the shop and put them in the right order for delivering on our own round. Often a policeman popped in for an early morning cup of tea. I had never done anything wrong in my life, but as we were brought up in such awe of the 'force', I always felt uncomfortable when he was there.

Every day my dog came with me on my paper round, and he knew it as well as I did. On wet days he would run ahead and shelter in the customer's doorway till I arrived, when he would move on to the next. He never got it wrong. I asked my dad *not* to let the dog out until he thought that I had already got my papers together and was out on the street. If the papers were late arriving and I was still in the shop when the dog was let out, to my great embarrassment he would come in and cock his leg up against the shop counter, and Mrs or Bob Irving would get very cross. I always tried to get my round finished before a certain family in Stanley Street let their large, vicious dog out, because it would always start a fight with mine. Dogs seem to reflect the character of their owners, and that one certainly did!

The last shop in the row was Mr Garwood's butcher's shop, on the corner with Queen Street. (It was later taken over by the Eastman chain of butchers.) On the other corner was a branch of the Consumers Tea Company, and almost opposite,

Bob Irving, the newsagent, in Russell Street.

in Queen Street, was a little electrical and wireless shop where accumulator batteries could be recharged. These batteries were used to power wireless sets (or radios) in the many households that still did not have electricity. When they ran down they would have to be taken somewhere for recharging, but because of their acid content they were not allowed on buses, which displayed notices saying that no accumulator batteries were to be carried on board.

In the main part of Russell Street was Ted Page's blacksmith's forge. Mr Page had done his apprenticeship with Mr Clarke, the blacksmith in Dane Street, and I believe he worked at that forge until it was demolished to make way for a shopping area. When I was twelve or thirteen, my dad let me take the light horses to Dane Street to be shod. I would have been very proud to take the shire as well (and being five feet eight inches tall already, I felt quite big enough to do so), but Dad was always very safety conscious and wouldn't let me.

There was a post office in Park Road East, and on Saturday mornings, when I was very young, my great-granddad used to take me with him when he went to collect his old age pension. He always bought me a penny bar of Cadbury's Milk Chocolate, and a tuppenny bar of plain chocolate to take home to my bedridden great-granny.

On the opposite side of the road, on the corner with Salisbury Street, was a front-room chemist's shop. The chemist was a small, elderly, white-haired man, who I believe was called Mr Matthews. The room was dimly lit by gaslight and furnished with a glass wall cabinet, a counter, and a bentwood chair to sit on whilst he mixed your medicine or rolled out pills on a grooved metal board made especially for the purpose. The Dickensian setting fired my imagination, and I would eagerly volunteer to go on errands to that chemist's shop.

My first recollection of a milkman was Albert Readman from Foster Hill Road, who brought milk to the door in churns, on a hand cart, and ladled it out – with a half or pint measure – into our own jug.

The knife grinder regularly visited the street on his push-bike. He would set up his cycle and pedal away to turn the grindstone. The blades would sing and sparks would fly as he sharpened knives, shears and scissors.

During the Depression in the 1930s, unemployed people sometimes walked down the middle of the streets singing and picking up the pennies which were thrown to them from bedroom windows.

Garfield Street is the proud possessor of a blue plaque: number 70 is the birthplace of comedian Ronnie Barker, the larger half of 'The Two Ronnies'. Ronnie and his parents moved away while he was still a toddler, but I remember Ronnie's grandparents, the Carters, who continued to live there, together with his Aunt Doll. They were a quiet, old-fashioned family, who seemed to be straight from the Victorian countryside. His grandfather would lean on the front gate and chat to neighbours and passers-by. Ronnie's Aunt Doll remained a spinster for some time, but she eventually married a very pleasant country man.

There were acres of allotments in the Black Tom area and

these were rented out by the council in plots of ten poles (about three hundred square yards). Nearly every householder rented one or more plots. Before the war, the land behind St Martin's Church and Clapham Road School, all the way up to Manton's Lane, was set out as allotments, until the Bedford Modern School acquired it for a second playing field. The allotment holders were given notice and left their plots. A neighbour took me fossicking for soft fruits on the abandoned allotments, but we were unlucky, and all we found were a few puny strawberries. War was imminent and the ground was ploughed up and set with cereals for the war effort; it didn't become a playing field until a number of years after the war had ended.

Stretches of allotments also ran from the back of the old Modern School playing field and Park Road North up to Manton's Lane (and what is now Brickhill Drive) and beyond, till they reached the fields of Clapham Park. The furthest plots, near Hoo Farm (usually called 'the Waterworks farm'), were much larger, and people farmed them as smallholdings, often with a few pigs or chickens; others were sown with wheat or barley.

My dad rented one of these plots, where he kept pigs and poultry, and, in summer, turned the horses out to graze. His pigsties were mostly made from old doors and windows, and the roofs from corrugated iron. The muck-heap matured so well over the years that he said it 'cut like butter', and from time to time he would cart some away to be dug into the soil on his vegetable plot. In the barn at the end he kept the pig meal, and the copper for boiling up the pigswill. On cold winter days we retired to the barn and sat round the boiler to keep warm – it's surprising how the smell of boiling pigswill can give you an appetite!

Cecil Daniel had the plot on one side, where he grazed his horses, and Mr Perrin had the plot on the other side. On one occasion my friends and I had borrowed an air rifle and were shooting at tins perched on the barn roof. We didn't see Mr Perrin working in his field until we heard him yell, 'Are you bl***y well trying to kill me?'

There was no piped water on any of the allotments, and it was essential for keeping animals, so Dad dug a well and lined it with forty-gallon molasses drums (minus the tops and bottoms). The water was hauled up with a bucket on a rope. The well was covered with a wooden lid, but as it was at ground level Dad was adamant that we never played near it.

The most diligently tended allotments, with no vacant plots, were at the top of Cemetery Hill, on the right-hand side, behind the cemetery. These stretched as far as Brightman's Spinney to the north and Brightman's Farm to the east. No one seemed to keep pigs or chickens on these plots, so perhaps they were not allowed to do so. As well as this large acreage, there were still more allotments at Cut Throat Lane.

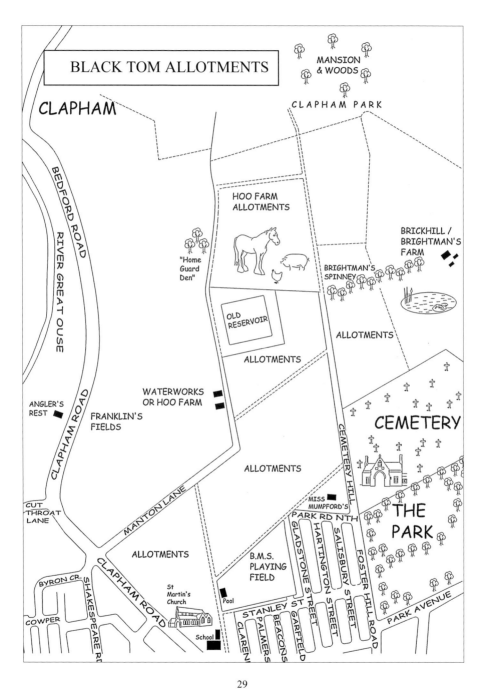

BLACK TOM ALLOTMENTS

CLAPHAM

MANSION & WOODS

CLAPHAM PARK

BEDFORD ROAD

RIVER GREAT OUSE

HOO FARM ALLOTMENTS

"Home Guard Den"

BRICKHILL / BRIGHTMAN'S FARM

BRIGHTMAN'S SPINNEY

OLD RESERVOIR

ALLOTMENTS

ALLOTMENTS

ANGLER'S REST

CLAPHAM ROAD

FRANKLIN'S FIELDS

WATERWORKS OR HOO FARM

CEMETERY HILL

CEMETERY

CUT THROAT LANE

MANTON LANE

ALLOTMENTS

MISS MUMPFORD'S

PARK RD NTH

THE PARK

GLADSTONE STREET

HARTINGTON STREET

SALISBURY STREET

FOSTER HILL ROAD

BYRON CR.

CLAPHAM ROAD

ALLOTMENTS

St Martin's Church

B.M.S. PLAYING FIELD

Pool

STANLEY ST

GARFIELD

SHAKESPEARE RD

COWPER

School

CLARENCE

PALMERS

BEACONS

PARK AVENUE

The author and cousin Maureen playing in the coal yard, 1937.

2

PLAYTIME

I spent all my youth in Black Tom and joined in the usual children's activities. In the spring our favourite pastime was 'primrosing'. We would set off up Cemetery Hill, along the footpath past the allotments, and through Clapham Park to Mansion Woods. Although there was a sign nailed to a tree which told us that 'Trespassers will be Prosecuted', we took no notice and came away with arms full of primroses or bluebells. We had learned how to recognise the horse chestnut by the horseshoe marks on its twigs, and we collected its 'sticky buds' and took them to school. Every classroom had vases of them on the windowsills, and over the weeks we watched them turn into leaves.

Going to or from the woods we could turn off the footpath into Brightman's Spinney, where there was a pedestal monument in memory of Algernon Foster of Brickhill House. He was born in Brickhill in 1811, but died in Dresden, Germany, in 1821, aged ten. We came out of the spinney into Brightman's Field, which had a pond where we collected newts and tadpoles. The pond is still there, but is now little more than a scruffy puddle between Brickhill Drive and

Rooksmead. We also collected birds' eggs, and learned to recognise the species by their size, colour and markings. A needle was inserted into each end of an egg and the yolk blown out before it was added to a collection. We were told it was perfectly all right to collect them if we took only one egg from each nest – how many children found the same nest doesn't bear thinking about.

At Easter no shops opened on Good Friday, but early in the morning someone came round the streets hawking hot cross buns. I remember my dad calling out of the bedroom window to order a dozen. On Easter Monday, Dad took us by rail to the London Cart Horse Parade. In May we looked forward to Elstow's May Day festival, with the procession of the May queen and her attendants, the maypole, and country dancing on the village green. Sandy Flower Show was very popular and on most people's summer agenda. My dad also took us by bus to the horse shows at Ampthill Park.

To fund their new indoor swimming pool, the Bedford Modern School held summer fetes in their playing field. From our front bedroom window I could see various marquees and the helter-skelter. All day long a loudspeaker belted out 'Little Sir Echo' and, young as I was, I managed to learn all the words.

When the swimming pool was finished the public could use it, out of school hours, at sixpence (2.5p) a time. It was always crowded. We young girls would take sandwiches, which we ate in the dressing room, so that we need not go home for tea. The yearly season ticket was excellent value at ten shillings and sixpence (52.5p). Unfortunately, many of us caught verrucas from the duckboards and from the wooden staircase which led to and from the ladies' dressing room.

On Sunday evenings in the summer we, as a family, would go for a stroll: up Cemetery Hill, past the allotments into Clapham Park, down Green Lane and back along Clapham Road. Our treat was to stop and have a drink at the Angler's Rest on the way home. My dad and my Uncle Alf would bring Golden Lemon drinks into the garden for their women and children before returning to the bar. One year, probably 1938, when we came through Clapham Park, we saw a camp of tents which I believed housed Jewish refugees – but they did not stay long.

We looked forward to trips to the seaside with the North End Club, which, combined with the other working men's clubs, the band clubs and the Trades Club, organized excursions by rail. These trains carried up to eight hundred people to places like Great Yarmouth; but Southend-on-Sea was our family's favourite.

At one end of the beach a couple of old-fashioned bathing machines could still be found. The sands were poor, being in a river estuary, but we paddled in the sea, walked down the mile -long pier (my dad would never pay for us to ride on the little train), spent our money at the Kursaal Gardens Amusement Park and had sausage and mash with fried onions at one of the many sea-front establishments – the smell was so enticing that meal times couldn't come too soon.

Another destination was Skegness, with its famous clock tower which appeared on all the souvenirs. The tide went out a long way, and deep gullies of water were left along the beach. In various places a little bridge on wheels was drawn up in the gulley so that you could cross to another part of the beach without getting your feet wet. My Uncle Alf was sure that 'them beggars dig the 'oles out just to make money', because they charged a penny to use the bridge. We children thought it would be fun to walk across the bridge, but we had to follow our adults, who wouldn't pay, and walk the long way round to get to the sea.

It was always windy at 'Skeggy', and Uncle Alf lost his brand-new trilby hat when it was blown out to sea. My aunt tried to catch it and followed it until the water reached her knickers, but the hat rolled along the surface on its brim until it was well out of reach.

Waiting in the railway carriage at Skegness station ready to go home, we became anxious when my dad and my uncle were still not on board and the train was about to leave. Uncle Alf had gone back into town to buy a mouth organ and my dad had gone with him. The guard was ready with his flag and whistle when I, a tearful seven year old, leaned out of the window and begged him not to blow his whistle and leave my daddy behind. I was crying as the train pulled out of the station, and my mum and my aunt were as mad as hatters. Then two young chaps came in from another carriage and started chatting them up. I was lying along the length of the bench seat when one of them sat on the end next to my mum. I tried to push him off with my feet, but didn't succeed. Suddenly Dad and Uncle Alf, who had managed to catch the train after all, arrived at their seats and were not best pleased at seeing their places usurped by two young men. A fight was

Gladys, Violet and Jim Tompkins at Southend-on-Sea.

Skegness 1939. Back: Charles 'Waggle' Brace. Second row: Hilda Brace, Alf Hills, Irene Hills, Jim Tompkins, Gladys Tompkins. Front row: Brian Brace, Yvonne Hills, Violet Tompkins.

about to break out; my mum and aunt tried to restrain their menfolk, whilst the other two made a hasty retreat to their own carriage. The women's temporary euphoria turned to anger when they discovered that their husbands had boarded the last coach of the very long train in good time, but had stopped to chat and have a drink with everyone they knew as they slowly made their way to their seats along the seemingly endless corridors. All the way back to Bedford you could have cut the atmosphere with a knife, even though Uncle Alf tried to relieve the tension by playing his new mouth organ. I was just glad to have my daddy back. That was the last rail excursion before the war started; when it ended we went on coach trips instead.

In the autumn, each armed with a chunk of wood, we children went in search of horse chestnut trees to pelt at. We had to be vigilant not to be struck on the head by another kid's piece of wood as it descended to the ground. Sometimes we would be too early, and the conkers would come out of their shells pale and unripe; but when they were perfectly ready they shone like burnished bronze. A hole was made through the middle with a butcher's metal skewer, and a leather bootlace with a knot in one end was threaded through. It was then ready to play 'conkers'. Some soaked theirs in vinegar to make them stronger. We would often claim we had a 'sixer' even though it was the conker's first time out.

Two or three weeks later, we made effigies of Guy Fawkes (or dressed ourselves up instead) and collected pennies for the guy. When I was about five, my aunt Mabel, who was only a few years older, dressed me as a guy and we knocked on doors asking for 'A penny for the guy'. I carried a tin in which to collect the money. At one house, in upper Gladstone Street, the lady asked what we were going to do with the money. I promptly answered, 'We're going to put it in Mr Cooper's Christmas Club and get a chocolate selection box at Christmas!' When we left the doorstep, I got a clip round the ear from Mabel. 'Why didn't you keep your mouth shut and just rattle the tin?' she moaned. I had no idea anyone would expect the money should go to charity.

At Christmas we went carol singing in groups of three or four, and again the proceeds went to top up our Christmas club subscriptions. The Town Band came round the streets playing carols and collecting money for their good causes. Every Christmas they would stop under the street light by our house and play 'Under the Mistletoe Bough' for my bedridden great-grandmother.

When the snow came, we would take a large tin tray (if we didn't have a sledge) to the slopes of Franklin's Fields, opposite the Angler's Rest, and toboggan down. We really enjoyed it – even though some of us, who couldn't stop, ended up scratched and bleeding in the hedge at the bottom.

Armed with a broom and shovel, I earned pocket money by clearing snow from the pavements of householders who couldn't, or didn't want to, do it themselves. The going rate was tuppence a frontage. My best friend Irene and her younger brother were also in the business. On one occasion she thought I had poached a prospective customer of hers, so she hit me on the head with her broom. I saw a few stars and incurred an egg-shaped lump, but my mother rubbed my head and ignored the incident. I carried on clearing snow but kept to my own end of the street. Irene and I were always falling in and out. Many times I ran home and told my mum to hide because 'Irene's going to send her mum to bash you up!' My mother's philosophy was that while the parents were quarrelling about their children, the kids were making it up! She was right. Over sixty-five years later, Irene and I are still best friends.

Most of the butchers in Bedford had their own slaughterhouses, and Sharp's, on the corner of Stanley Street and Gladstone Street, was our nearest. On Saturday lunchtimes we would hang round the gates of Sharp's, waiting for them to unload the pigs or steers that had been bought at Bedford Cattle Market. Sometimes, although not often, during the unloading an animal would escape into the street. We scattered to avoid it – to us, of course, it was always a 'mad bull' or 'mad boar' however young and frightened the poor thing really was.

Every Saturday night, before 1940 when my Grandma Hills moved to Black Tom, her large family gathered together at her house in Pilcroft Street and my mother would take me to join them. We had a choice of two routes: one via the Town Bridge, and the other by the New Bridge in Prebend Street. When we went by way of the Town Bridge, we would stop at the market on St Paul's Square. All the stalls had Tilley lamps, which hissed and smelled and gave out a ghostly light. Dad would go to the second-hand book stall (which backed onto the railings of St Paul's churchyard and faced towards the Saracen's Head), where he would swap his Sexton Blake detective stories or Zane Grey cowboy books and buy comics for me. Then we would go to the cake stall facing Castle Lane and get a big bag of doughnuts, which at that time of night were sold at a reduced price to get rid of them. We bought a pint of winkles for Grandma before we continued down St Mary's and St John's Streets, past the Goat public house on the corner of Ampthill Street, and so to Grandma's house. I was fascinated by the way she used a pin to get the winkles out.

Sometimes we went to Grandma's by another route using Adelaide Square, with the prison wall on one side and the Girls' High School on the other. In the 1930s, painted in white on the prison wall, was a flash within a large circle and some wording – I can't remember what it said, and in any case I didn't understand it, but my mother said it had been done by the 'Blackshirts', who were fascists. The authorities had tried to clean it off, but could only manage to tone it down. It remained on the wall for a very long time.

Our route then continued down Gwyn Street, River Street (with the Salvation Army Citadel and its glass cupola) and towards the cattle market. On the corner where the Salvation Army now stands was an old cast-iron pissoir. We went through the cattle market, past the Birch Bus garage and the Commercial Baths and onto the New Bridge. If I remember rightly, we passed another cast-iron gents' urinal on the Black Diamond corner before we reached my grandmother's from that end of Cauldwell Street.

Our favourite all-year-round activity was going to the cinema. My cousin Eric first took me to the pictures when I was about four years old, and from then on I became a regular picture-goer. When he was not at school, we would go to the Empire – a small picture house near Woolworth's in Midland Road. We would arrive as soon as it opened and, having brought our sandwiches with us, stay until it was our bedtime.

Every Saturday morning there was a special cinema session for children. At first it was held at the Empire. The four-abreast queue extended past what was once Bedford's pawn shop (and later became Kelly's Milk Bar), round the corner into Allhallows Lane and as far back as Church Square (Pigeon Square). Regular attendees joined the 'Empire Children's Club' and received a badge and an attendance card, which was stamped when you bought your ticket. I can't remember what the prize was for a fully-stamped card. My favourite films were about Flash Gordon, Gene Autrey, and the Three Stooges.

With the influx of so many evacuees, the 'Saturday morning rush' was transferred to the much larger Granada Cinema in St Peter's Street, which was a beautiful Art-Deco building. It had a fantastic Wurlitzer theatre organ which was played by Johnny Uff. The stage was large enough to put on variety shows, and Brian Michie held his talent contest there. Before the Saturday morning films started, children shouted across the auditorium to friends and threw paper pellets and other missiles at them; sometimes fights broke out. The manager, Mr Blake (I believe), kept control of boisterous children with the aid of a long stick; but I never actually saw him in action. The lights went down, to the accompaniment of loud cheers, and the programme began. If there was any

The Empire Cinema in Midland Road. The Children's Saturday morning films were shown here in the 1930s.

The Picturedrome Cinema stood on St Mary's side of the river where the Moat House Hotel now stands. When the river was in flood and the water was approaching the cinema steps, a notice came on the screen advising the audience to evacuate the building.

soppy kissing in a film, the cinema echoed with hoots and jeers. The club became the 'Granadiers', although I never joined. I attended the Saturday morning screenings less and less, and left off completely when I was twelve.

During my elementary-school days, I accompanied Irene and her mother to the cinema several times a week. As well as the Empire and the Granada, there was the Plaza and the Picturedrome. The programmes were changed twice a week, so there were a lot of films to see. During the war they opened on Sundays as well. The father of the family who lived in the house opposite us was the commissionaire at the Plaza, and one of his sons worked at the Picturedrome. Every week they were supplied with free tickets, and I often went with the daughter, or one of the other members of the family, on their free ticket. Mr Hewitt, the grocer, displayed adverts for the Granada and Plaza cinemas in his shop window – this entitled him to two free tickets every week, and sometimes Mrs Hewitt took me with her for company. I think, over those years, I must have seen every film that was made.

The wireless (as we called the radio) played a big part in our lives. At first we listened to 'Children's Hour', presented by Uncle Mac, who read to us from 'Toytown' with its characters Larry the Lamb and Mr Grouser. We also listened to Romany the Gypsy with his nature-study talks. If we tuned to Luxembourg we could get 'The Ovaltinies' – a club for 'little girls and boys', as the advert said, who drank Ovaltine before they went to bed.

As we got older we listened to 'In Town Tonight', a topical events programme – but only because that was what our parents wanted; it was a bit too serious for children. We preferred the comedy programmes, such as Tommy Handley's 'ITMA' (It's That Man Again); 'Bandwaggon', with Arthur Askey and Richard 'Stinker' Murdoch; and 'Happidrome', whose title song went: 'We three in Happidrome, Working for the BBC, Ramsbottom and Enoch and me.' We learned all the songs and catch phrases. We enjoyed 'Monday Night at Eight O'clock', which had something for everyone; the plays on 'Saturday Night Theatre'; and Valentine Dyall as 'The Man in Black'.

During the war, light programmes especially tailored for each branch of the armed forces were broadcast, hosted by well-known comedians such as Charlie Chester. Everyone seemed to listen to 'The Radio Doctor', who had a slot just after eight in the morning. One piece of advice he gave to elderly people was to take a rest after they had evacuated their bowels. I thought this very amusing, and wondered where Grandma would like to have hers evacuated to – Southend or Skegness!

The fair was held twice a year on the open part of the cattle market opposite Battison Street. The showmen lived in large wooden caravans parked among the steam engines which powered the rides. Thick cables snaked along the ground. The noise, the smell of the machinery and the screams from people on the rides are memories one never forgets. There were the usual stalls such as hoop-la, which rarely seemed to give out a prize, and roll-a-penny, which I liked better because you could see for yourself whether you had won or not.

To test their strength, men could take a long-handled mallet and hit a block which sent a piece of metal shooting up a tall, measured length of wood. If it reached the top and rang the bell, the contestant was a winner. I never found out what they won, if anything, because the men were so busy congratulating themselves afterwards on their prowess. In a similar vein they would use the punchball. As a child I could never understand why anyone would want to pay to hit an old leather football hanging on a chain in an open booth with what appeared to be a clock at the back.

Darts players could test their skills throwing darts at playing cards, and on one occasion my Uncle Alf won a large cuddly toy as a prize. My dad was a good shot, but he never won anything on the rifle range and it was thought that most of the guns were rigged. There were bumper cars, where you were never allowed to bump; and Dodgems, on which you were obviously meant to dodge but always tried to bump – until told off by one of the tough-looking young attendants who showed off by expertly nipping from one moving car to another.

I never pestered my parents for goes on the rides, but occasionally I had a turn on the swing boats or the children's roundabout. When I was older, I had a ride on 'the Gallopers'. I was wearing a silk petticoat, and as the roundabout speeded up, I began to slip off the horse's back until I found myself hanging on for dear life. I was so scared of being thrown off that I couldn't even scream. I never went on one of those again. Fairs held no fascination for me, except when I was older and found it was a place to join up with friends and meet boys!

Most children joined the scout groups. I joined St Martin's Brownies in 1939. Standing around a large toadstool with other new recruits, I swore the Brownie oath and was enrolled into the Fairy pack. I was given a new pencil and a black notebook in which to record my good deeds. Second in command to Brown Owl was Tawny Owl. Ours worked at a dental surgery and was very keen on our dental hygiene. I was given a new toothbrush and a block of Gibbs Dentifrice. We were taught basic first aid, how to tie professional knots, sewing and darning, and how to send messages in Morse code and semaphore. I enjoyed my days with the Brownies; but when I had to move up to the Girl Guides I didn't take to it, and left before enrolment.

Bedford Park should have been our playground, but we preferred the streets. We played such games as hide-and-seek, statues, 'several men have come to work' and other kerb-to-kerb games. There were two types of hopscotch: the usual one of eight squares, normally made by the squares of the paving slabs, and another which was chalked on the road. This game started by drawing a circle marked 'home' in the middle of the road. A line drawn from it formed an ammonite shape and covered the road from kerb to kerb. This was chalked into sections, and if your stone landed on a section you marked it with your name; the next player had to hop over the marked square. The more squares marked with a name, the more difficult it was to reach 'home'. With very little traffic on the road, the game remained there until rain eventually washed it away.

It was usually the boys who tied neighbouring doorknobs together, knocked on the doors and waited to see the results. Ever mindful that the householders were usually customers of my dad, I steered clear of such activities. We girls enjoyed playing 'two balls' against a suitable wall, or skipping whilst chanting a variety of traditional skipping rhymes. Another popular game was playing 'fag cards' or 'flicks' – if the cigarette card you flicked covered one that had already been thrown, it was yours. The boys were much better at flicking than the girls, who usually lost their cards. It was the same with marbles, and boys were proud of their 'glass alleys'. Some marbles were very attractive with coloured glass threads running through the middle, the same as in some paperweights. Most girls kept them just for their beauty.

Games had their seasons, and in summer we played whip and top. The girls spent a lot of time decorating the tops with coloured chalks to create a kaleidoscope when spinning. There were two types of top: the 'mushroom' and the 'beehive'. The beehive had a better surface for decorating, but the mushroom gave a better performance. Between every kerbstone was a little hole where a top had been seated to make a start. By winding the whip lace round the shank of the top and giving it a sharp pull, it came out of the hole and started spinning in the road. The boys, once they had wound the string or shoelace (which made a better whiplash) round the top, preferred to send it whizzing through the air from their hands before it hit the ground spinning. Occasionally a top would spin into a windowpane – then, as if by magic, the street would be clear of children.

On every suitable wall, preferably away from windows, a set of wickets was chalked up and cricket practice took place. The boys didn't let the girls join in because the girls always bowled underarm. The ambition of every boy was to bowl a good overarm, and they could often be seen practising with an imaginary ball as they walked along the street.

With Foster Hill Cemetery being in our area, funeral processions often passed by. We always stopped playing, the boys took their caps off and we stood silently at the kerbside until it was out of sight.

Black Tom, like other areas of the town, had its colourful character, and ours was Peter Philips. Well known for his habit of picking up the 'dog-ends' of cigarettes and for the perpetual dewdrop on the end of his nose, he was teased unmercifully by boys. He would forestall the onslaught, or retaliate, by shouting at them.

Peter lived with his mother in Stanley Street. Mrs Philips, who usually dressed in a little black suit with a silver fox fur and a saucy cocked hat, looked like a faded Parisienne. She was a top-class dressmaker and made dresses for my mother and me. Her living room, where she used the table to do the cutting out, was rather dark and dingy, shaded by trees in the playing field; but the front room, with her sewing machine and tailors dummy, had a bay window and was much brighter.

Mrs Philips didn't get the clientele her skill deserved because the house reeked of cats and the boiled fish that they ate. Peter and his mother were true cat lovers. They took in any stray cat and had quite a number of them. Peter was often seen walking in the street with a cat in his arms. He had a full-time, albeit menial, job in his younger days, but in his later years he sold evening papers in the town. If he had copies left at the end of the day, he would trawl the pubs until he had sold them all.

Another character was Conga Dean, the local chimney sweep from Beaconsfield Street, who had a 'cock-eye'. When we saw him going into a house to clean the chimney, we would stand in the street waiting for the brush to emerge from the pot and in unison call, 'It's out! It's out!' During the war, Mr Dean was called up, cock-eye or not, into the Pioneer Corps (I believe), and the area was deprived of its sweep.

A neighbour had a new set of sweep's brushes and my dad asked him to clean our chimney. However, it turned out to be an unfortunate and expensive venture – the neighbour didn't realize he had to keep turning his brush in the same direction and it came undone and stuck in the chimney. The offending brush-head would not let the smoke go up the chimney, so Mr Catlin, the nearby builder, had to be employed to remove some bricks from high up on the outside wall and retrieve the brush.

At Christmas time Maurice Barker (also from Beaconsfield Street) would come and wring the necks of the cockerels my dad had 'brought on' for sale at that time of year. Chicken was a luxury usually eaten only at Christmas. Maurice would sit in our stables to pluck the fowls, then, when only the fine 'hairs' were left on them, he would come into the kitchen and, with the flames from the ring of the gas stove, singe them off the carcasses. It created a pungent smell that was unforgettable.

Another memorable character was the refined elderly lady who lived at the corner of Stanley Street and the top half of Salisbury Street. She looked like a duchess, dressed in the fashion of Queen Alexandra or Queen Mary, with her white hair piled high on her head and a choker at her neck. She owned a cockatoo, which often sat in the bay window of her front room. Sometimes she stood at her front gate with the bird on her hand and she would let us stroke it.

Although we usually played in the street, we would go to Bedford Park to play on the swings. They were at the very east end of the park, at what was then the edge of the town. It seemed quite a trek, especially for children from Clarendon or Palmerston Street. We could never time it right to leave for home and were usually late for our meals.

My favourite dinner was a beef pudding, cooked in a basin, which made its own delicious gravy. Sometimes we would have a bacon and onion 'clanger' (a long suet pudding) – probably not the original Bedfordshire clanger, which was supposed to have jam at one end, although I never knew of anyone who actually made or ate one of those. The sweet course would have been a separately-cooked jam 'roly-poly' pudding or spotted dick. Both the clanger and the puddings were cooked in the same way: wrapped in cloth, tied twice round the middle – at a third and two-thirds of its length – and boiled all morning. It was usually a heavy, solid pudding which left no room for second helpings.

'The swings' was a dangerous place. The playground was covered in gravel and all the equipment was placed on concrete paving slabs. When one child got off the seesaw, the other, left in the air, would come crashing down onto the slab, bounce, be shot off, and usually land on its head. It's a wonder we didn't all have brain damage. The roundabout could go at a tremendous rate and little children, in the charge of brothers or sisters, were often shot into space.

There were 'flying swings', which consisted of a telegraph pole topped with a rotatable cone (shaped like a coolie hat) from which hung about a dozen stout seven-foot-long chains, each with a wooden handlebar at the end. You had to stretch up to reach a handlebar (shorter children were lifted up to clutch the bars), then, running round as fast as you could, you would be swung out by centrifugal force and 'fly' through the air. Often the older boys would let go in mid flight and jump out of the way, which left their wooden handles swinging free

A very early picture of the 'flying swings' at the east end of Bedford Park.

to hurtle at the heads of the remaining hangers-on. To avoid them you let go and landed heavily in the gravel, sustaining cuts and bruises. There were two of these lethal weapons in the playground.

The sets of ordinary swings were in different sizes to cope with all ages. There was also a set of parallel bars, which no one knew how to use properly. On opposite sides of the playground were rustic shelters, which were reminiscent of Swiss chalets. Their wooden panels were covered with the carvings of hearts and the initials of lovers.

Outside the entrance to the swings, and adjacent to the park's lake, was the aviary. The most popular cage was the one with the peacock. We always hoped he would display his tail when we stopped to look at him. Other pens held exotic types of pheasants and very pretty Indian game birds. These were all taken away at the beginning of the Second World War. The ducks on the lake remained an attraction, especially when they had ducklings, but rats were their predators and many little ones were lost.

In the thick borders of laurel bushes we created 'dens'. If you entered another gang's den, a fight would break out. We were warned to beware of 'old men in the bushes', but no one ever suggested that young men might be just as dangerous.

As little girls we preferred to go to the bowling green, which was surrounded by park benches. We would sit quietly and play with dolls, or make chains from daisies collected in the park. We must have been an unwanted distraction for the 'serious' bowls players and sometimes they sent us away.

At the north end of the drive, near the bowling green, was

the park's café. Its interior was very spartan, but we thought it would be rather grand to have tea there. It always seemed to be empty – but perhaps on Sunday afternoons, when we were at Sunday school, it came into its own.

The café sold ices, and if we were lucky we could buy a halfpenny Lyons ice cream. These ice creams seem to have been made in the form of a pole, like a broom handle, protected by a thin cardboard sheath and cut off at intervals of about an inch. The penny version was a bit thicker. The halfpenny ice had a wooden cocktail stick poked into the centre to hold it by, but the penny one was supposed to be put into a wafer cone. Sometimes we found the shopkeeper would put that on a stick as well, no doubt to save himself the cost of a cone, but we never dared complain. We were always fascinated by the ice-cream delivery van with its clouds of 'smoke' created by the dry ice (solid carbon dioxide) packed around the boxes. Sometimes the driver would give us each a small piece of this smoking substance which we studied in wonder: how could something so cold actually smoke and also burn your fingers?

At the other end of the drive, on a grass verge, was the bandstand. We rarely saw a band, but again it probably played on Sunday afternoons when we were not there. Behind the bandstand were the tennis courts. These were netted at the back near the bushes, where it would have been difficult to find stray balls, but the other side was open to the grass verge and the passing public. One summer evening, when I was about six years old and on my own, I watched a set of doubles playing. When a loose ball came my way, I returned it. At the end of the session the players packed up and gave me a halfpenny each for being ball boy – so I earned tuppence, the going rate for a week's pocket money! It wasn't easy getting to be a ball-boy because the older children, who were known to fight amongst themselves to cover a court, always saw us younger ones off.

Several cricket matches would take place in the park at the same time, and we felt we ought to sit and watch them. Eventually utter boredom drove us off. When no matches were taking place, we enjoyed rolling down the incline in front of the cricket pavilion to see which of us could roll the furthest. Some of us learned to ride our bikes down that slope – it was much easier to keep your balance when coasting than when pedalling.

In the bushes behind the cricket pavilion was a cast-iron gents' urinal. Like all children we were fascinated by other people's lavatories, and this one was no exception. The surrounding bushes made it dark and eerie, and it smelt terrible, but when no one was there the girls took a peep inside to see what it was like. It was disgusting!

Attached to the back of the keeper's house, opposite De Parys Avenue and next to the council's nurseries and greenhouses, were the ladies' lavatories. There were two or three toilet cubicles, but the place was dark and dank and uninviting. Built into the outside wall was a type of sink or trough with a water tap and, on a chain, a drinking cup made of a grey metal which was encrusted with what seemed to be little barnacles. We never risked it near our mouths and preferred to drink out of our cupped, if somewhat dirty, hands.

Bedford Park.

Near the swings, at the other keeper's cottage, was a toilet which appeared to be his own outside lavatory and which was the only one in the park fit for ladies to use. No doubt there was one at the café, but we children never used it.

The grass in the park was cut with a gang mower and deposited in heaps for collection, probably to be composted at the council's nursery garden. During my school dinner hour, when I was about eight years old, one of my duties was to go to the park to fill a sack with cut grass. My dad gave me strict instructions not to collect it from heaps which children had played in because that caused the grass to heat up. I brought it straight home on the crossbar of my bike and spread it out on the well-swept concrete in our yard, so that it could wilt before being fed to the horses.

We all respected the park ranger, who patrolled the park on his bike wearing his uniform of riding breeches and knee-high leather gaiters. He was dispensed with when war broke out.

The author, aged 14, in Dutch national dress, taken when the Harpur Central School went to Holland in 1946.

3

SCHOOL DAYS

I started at Clapham Road Mixed School at Easter 1937, when I was five years old. The first year at the Infants' School was taken by Miss Blake and known as the 'babies' class'. The main feature in her classroom was a large, three-seater rocking horse, which stood in front of the unlit fireplace. On rare occasions children were allowed a ride in the seats at either end of the rocker; a very lucky one sat astride the horse itself. I can't remember ever having a ride. I was much taller, and therefore heavier, than any of the other children, and so there was no one who would have balanced me in the seat at the other end. I was not lucky enough to be offered the horse's back.

We sat in pairs at blonde wood tables with matching chairs. These were set out, as were all the desks throughout the school, in rows which were divided into four blocks, with girls on one side of the class and boys on the other. The least able children were seated at the front of the class, which graduated in ability towards the back where the brightest pupils sat. During that first year, a little girl who sat in the row in front of me often wet her knickers; we dreaded being moved into her chair.

We were each given a small cardboard box containing a bean bag, to help us with co-ordination; some cowry shells, with which to learn to count; a stick of chalk, to use on a slate or chalkboard; and a duster to rub it off again. Once a week we used plasticine. The monitor gave out sheets of white cardboard, measuring about eight inches by six, with a dot marked at each corner and another in the middle. Then, with green plasticine, we made candles and stuck one on each of the dots. Having accomplished this great task, the plasticine (I can still conjure up its smell) was rolled back into a ball and, with the boards, collected up until the following week when the whole procedure was repeated. Artistic licence was not on the curriculum.

May 12th, 1937, was the Coronation Day of King George VI and Queen Elizabeth. Celebrations were held at Mill Meadows, and the Town Band played from a floating platform on the river. We were given a day off school, a coronation mug, and a book of tickets to be used at the celebrations.

That afternoon my dad took me to the children's party held in the Meadows. One of the tickets was for our tea; we queued up and received a bottle of school milk and a small paper carrier bag with string handles, in which we found a sticky bun and a halfpenny finger of Cadbury's milk chocolate. The other tickets were for rides on the fun fair. We could also take a turn on the miniature railway, which ran regularly in the Meadows, or have a trip on the river steamer which was boarded from the steps by the side of the Town

Bridge, near the Swan Hotel. On the opposite bank, adults could hire punts or rowing boats from Chetham's Boathouse; there were pedal boats for children at Longholme.

Nearly every street held its own coronation party. My mother decided to dress up for ours and wore a Victorian outfit that had belonged to my great-great-grandmother Mahalah. She was amused to find that her 'disguise' was so effective that several of our neighbours failed to recognise her.

Most of the town's celebrations or community events took place in Russell Park, which was more central than Bedford Park. But in the 1930s, a tattoo or night-time pageant about the British Empire was held in Bedford Park. I went to see it with my mother and we sat on uncomfortable, folding park chairs, made of cast iron with wooden slats forming the seats. I couldn't see much of the floodlit show from my seat, but I waited patiently for the firework display which was to follow. Halfway through the evening I needed a 'wee-wee'. It was dark, so my mother took me into the bushes to relieve myself. As we ventured into the undergrowth we found ourselves in the middle of a group of Zulu warriors wearing grass skirts and carrying spears and shields. I don't know who was more scared, my mother or me. I can't remember having a wee, but I can vividly remember the Zulus (who were, of course, soldiers dressed up for the part). The firework display was quite spectacular for its time, and ended with blazing pictures of the King and Queen's faces above the words 'God Save the King'.

On special days, the headmistress of the Infants' School,

During the Coronation celebrations a band played from this bandstand floating on the river.

Gladys Tompkins dressed up in Great Grandma Mahalah's costume for Garfield Street's 1937 Coronation party.

Garfield Street's 1937 Coronation Party. The author is second child on far left. Mrs Daniel with her daughter Janet in the pram.

Coronation 1937. Garfield Street top end. Standing L to R: Old Mrs Johnson, Gladys Tompkins, Mrs Puplet, Mr Puplet, Young Mrs Johnson (Nellie). Seated L to R: Old Mr Johnson and Loammi Tompkins.

Miss Hopkins, who was an officer in the Red Cross, would wear her smart, navy-blue uniform to take assembly in the school hall. Every Armistice Day, on November 11th, we assembled at eleven o'clock in the morning and kept the two-minute silence; even the youngest child managed it. In 1938, when Mr Chamberlain returned from Germany with his 'piece of paper', we assembled to give thankful prayers for 'peace in our time'.

My second year at school was spent in Miss Roger's class. She was a lovely teacher, quite young, who taught us how to read, and to write in an exercise book rather than on a chalkboard. This classroom was part of the school hall, which was divided into two classrooms by floor-to-ceiling, glass-panelled wooden folding doors. The room on the other side was occupied by the third year and taught by Miss Cook.

Miss Cook had taught my father when he was a boy, and hers was my next and last class in the Infants' School. She taught us how to use pen and ink and to do joined-up writing. When reading round the class, she would pick pupils at random to continue the story. Perhaps it was not really at random but children who were staring out of the window or glazing over. We also learned art and handicrafts. We drew in crayon and painted in watercolour. The boys made raffia teapot stands, whilst the girls made little raffia bags or learned to knit by making dishcloths on huge needles with white string. We also made pen wipers out of felt or old coat-cloth. They consisted of three or four layers of four-inch-square material kept together by a button sewn through the middle. We all had one to keep our pen nibs clean.

In this class we started doing PT, or 'physical jerks' as we called it, every morning in the playground, weather permitting. With our skirts tucked into our navy-blue knickers, we drilled with a lot of bending and stretching. The apparatus work consisted of balancing and walking on the narrow strut of an upturned bench. Sometimes we had team events, and each team was identified by a red, yellow, blue or green band worn across the shoulder to the waist.

In May of that year (1939) a National Defence Parade and recruiting drive took place in Russell Park which attracted crowds of people, and we children found it very exciting. There were soldiers, women in army uniform and many interesting things to see, including an army tank which we were allowed to climb into. We had never seen servicewomen before, and I immediately abandoned my ambition to be an engine-driver and wanted to become a lady soldier instead. Before we went home we played on the old Crimean cannon gun, burnished bright over the years by boys' trousers and little girls' knickers, which stood on the grass verge of the Embankment, opposite Russell Park. It had always been a great source of fun; but the cannon, like the garden railings, disappeared when the war started.

Miss Cook asked us to write about what we wanted to do when we grew up, and enthused by what I had seen at the rally in Russell Park, I wrote that I wanted to be a lady soldier and fight with guns. She asked me to stay behind after school, when she explained that lady soldiers didn't fight with guns but mended the soldiers' socks and cooked their meals! No doubt she saw things differently in the years that followed. As seven-year-olds we seemed to have come a long way in Miss Cook's class.

We celebrated Empire Day at Clapham Road School. The date, May 24th, had been chosen because it was Queen Victoria's birthday. The maypole was often in use in the playground, with dancers rehearsing for the big day when it would be set up on the lawn in front of the school. On Empire Day we would line up class by class in the playground, and march down the path, through the infants and girls' gate, along the footpath in Clapham Road and through the boys' gate. We passed in front of the school building, and, as we did so, we saluted the two mighty horse chestnut trees that grew in the lawn which swept down to the road. The trees were named 'Ladysmith' and 'Mafeking', after the South African towns which were besieged in the autumn of 1899 and relieved in February and May 1900. They were probably planted to mark those events. Perhaps we were meant to have been aiming our salutes at the nearby flagpole with its Union Jack, but it was the trees that actually received them.

After singing patriotic songs, we sat cross-legged on the lawn and watched the maypole dancing. I longed for the time when I would be old enough to participate, but events decided that it was not to be; I can't remember Empire Day being kept at the school after 1939.

In the early summer we were encouraged to compete in the Elementary Schools' Sports Day. The infants' classes competed in the running and in the three-legged and sack races. The sports were held at the rugby football ground in Goldington Road. The official programmes, which cost

Dancing round the Maypole on the front lawn of Clapham Road School (Livingstone School) c. 1930.

thruppence I believe, were in the form of booklets, with places to record the winners of the heats and finals.

Sitting on the ground, we watched the events. With all of Bedford's elementary schools taking part, there were many heats for every event before the finals took place. We had to attend as it was considered part of the school day, but for many of us it was incredibly boring. The little picnics we took with us helped to relieve the boredom. The sports day was discontinued when war broke out, to the relief of many of the non-competitors.

At the outbreak of the war, Clapham Road School took in 674 evacuee pupils, mostly from Islington, Holloway, Camden and Kentish Town. We were given two weeks' extra summer holiday. Officially this was to give local children a chance to get to know the evacuees who were billeted with them before the new term began. A more likely explanation was that it gave the Education Committee more time to sort out the problems associated with having such a vast influx of children.

When I returned to school I moved up into Standard One, which was not considered to be in the infants any more although the classroom was still in the infants' building. We were taught by another pleasant and excellent teacher, Miss Reynolds, who was also one of my dad's customers (although this didn't win me any special favours). We were all pleased and proud to be going into Standard One, but when we got there it was not what we expected. We found the classroom filled with all sorts of equipment, including a large weaving loom from one of the evacuated schools. We never saw it in use and it was eventually taken away.

The biggest change was to the school curriculum. We could only use the classrooms from 9.00 a.m. until 12.00 noon and the evacuees used them from 1.30 p.m. to 4.30 p.m. Every afternoon during that warm and pleasant autumn we went on nature study walks, in what was then the nearby countryside, and collected specimens of wild flowers, leaves and berries. We started in the lane at the side of the school (now Slade Walk), which ran through the allotments and lead by way of a small gateway at the far end into Manton's Lane. We turned right, continued past the Waterworks farm, across Hoo Farm allotment smallholdings (now Murdock Road), returning by way of Cemetery Hill, over the stile and down the dirt footpath (Gainsborough Rise, Hogarth Close and Landseer Walk) – taking care to avoid the mud made by an ever-running spring on one of the allotments behind Miss Mumford's nursing home for unmarried mothers, off Park Road North – then past the Modern School playing field and swimming bath and back to school, where we were dismissed for the day.

When winter came we spent the afternoons in St Martin's Church Hall, which was next to the school. It was hired by the Education Committee for fifty shillings (£2.50) a week. We were packed in like sardines. Our damp outdoor clothing caused a cloud of vapour to form near the ceiling. At first there were too many of us to take any form of lessons. We sat as best we could in classes, and listened to stories. The girls did a lot of French knitting on cotton reels which had four shoe nails hammered into one end; by using a hairpin to loop the wool over the nails, they made the stitches. The yards of tubular knitting they produced were made into reins for toddlers or stitched into coils to make cushion covers. Later, desks were moved into the church hall and arranged to form open-plan classrooms. Our education continued in this way until we were able to go back to the school buildings full time. By then we were happily integrated with the evacuee pupils and back to a proper school timetable.

Jewish and Roman Catholic children didn't receive any religious instruction at school, and Church of England pupils took theirs next door in St Martin's Church. On Tuesday and Friday mornings over a hundred children attended. St Martin's was High Church in its traditions and it was also my parish church. I had attended the Sunday school when I was younger, and I attended Mass conducted by Father Eddington on Sunday mornings, and catechism with the curate Father Smith in the afternoons.

In that year (1939–1940) Miss Reynolds had fifty-two pupils in Standard One. As usual, the rows of desks were divided into blocks with the clever ones at the back and the least able at the front, but this time each block became a team, with its own colour and a board on which to register its achievements. For good work we were given appropriately coloured stars, and at the end of the week the stars on the boards were added up to see which was the best team.

In Standard One we took our first end-of-term tests and had our first school report. I was glad the report didn't include handicrafts. Miss Reynolds must have despaired at my attempt to knit a tea cosy. I always put a plain stitch where a purl stitch should have been and vice versa. She had to undo so much of my work to correct it that she eventually gave it to June Beechy to finish for me. During that term June had already knitted herself a long woollen vest before doing most of my tea cosy.

In the autumn, as juniors, we went up to the 'Big School'. The building was very similar to the Infants' School except that it had classrooms leading from both sides of the main hall. We assembled in our respective classes in the playground and marched smartly into the school hall to the music of Sousa played on a gramophone. The headmaster, 'Titch' Northern, took assembly and, after prayers, informed us where the latest battles of the war were taking place. He marked them on a map with coloured pins, which helped me with my geography.

My first teacher in the 'Big School' was the dreaded Miss Careless. Her reputation had put the fear of the devil in us before we ever came into contact with her. She gave me my first taste of the cane. On that occasion we were singing, standing with our hands behind our backs. I leaned forward and gently tugged on the cardigan of the girl in front; I was spotted and given the cane.

Miss Careless taught us how to sew. I hated it, but with a lot of help I made a very basic nightdress case. The only enjoyable thing in her class was the story she read to us on Friday afternoons.

At morning break we bought a bottle of milk with a halfpenny ticket purchased from the milk monitor. In winter the bottles were often frozen solid and had to be brought indoors and put beside the radiators to thaw out. We kept the cardboard bottle tops – washed and dried, they were used as templates to make woollen pom-poms.

As juniors we were allowed to go swimming with the school to the Commercial Baths – not a pleasant experience. The open-air, river-water baths had wooden changing rooms on the side of the pool which were always cold and damp. I don't think the sun ever reached over the high wooden fence which surrounded the pool. The non-swimmers' or learners' area was railed off at one corner. Below the waterline, the blue-grey non-porous bricks were green and slimy with river algae and very slippery. I got out of attending as often as I could, and I didn't learn to swim!

The next class up from Miss Careless's must have been quite uneventful, because I cannot remember who took it – only that we were taught in one half of the divided school hall. The class on the other side of the partition was taken by one of only two schoolmasters, Mr Rogers. He was a very pleasant man, but I was never in his class.

Occasionally, to our joy, the hall was opened up in the afternoon and we had film shows. They were mild propaganda shorts about war savings, digging for victory, keeping healthy and the theme 'Careless talk costs lives'. Films like the ones demonstrating that 'coughs and sneezes spread diseases' were often given a comical twist as well as carrying the serious message. I found the most interesting films were the ones about farming, showing horses ploughing the fields and sheaves of corn being fed into threshing drums. The music which accompanied the commentary was my earliest introduction to the classics.

I was in Miss Kendall's for my last year at Clapham Road School and did very well in her class. We took an assessment test to see if we were worthy to sit the eleven-plus for the Harpur Trust schools. Although I qualified to sit, I was given no idea what to expect or how to tackle the exam paper. I sat the exam at the Bedford High School and was completely overawed by my surroundings. When I got the chance to take the Harpur Trust Central School exam, I was more prepared and passed. There were two eleven-plus classes at Clapham Road and the pupils in Miss Newbold's class were thought to be the brightest, but in our class a boy from London passed for the Bedford Modern School when he was nine years old.

Miss Clarke was the senior mistress at Clapham Road School and taught the final year girls who left school at the age of fourteen. She was also the teacher who administered punishment (which was always the cane) to the girls. If you were late for school once, Miss Clarke gave you one stroke of the cane on one hand; late twice, you got one stroke on both hands, and so on through the week. In those days we all went home for dinner, so that was another chance to be late back. By the end of the week, very bad timekeepers had very sore hands. I had to give up calling for my friend Irene because she was seldom ready, and waiting for her made me late and I got the cane too.

In September 1943, I moved to the Harpur Trust Central School in Horn Lane. The headmaster was Mr A. B. Wignall. Boys and girls were taught in separate buildings, and having come from a mixed school I liked the idea of single-sex

CLAPHAM ROAD SCHOOL: THE 11 PLUS YEAR, JULY 1943.

Top Row L to R: Dennis Swannel, Michael Green, Derek Farr, Clifford Greenaway, Daphne Hyde, John Frazer, Michael Butler, Royston Stevens(?), George Craven.

Standing L to R: Violet Tompkins, Pamela Appleby, Audrey Lett, Margaret Bliss, Marian Davis, Rosemary Mantel, Joan Denton, Sylvia Brooks, Muriel Thacker, Jean Ward, Yvonne Stein, Daphne Lett, Iris Patterson.

Seated L to R: Miss Newbold, Brenda Benford, Mary Asher, Violet Walker, Maureen Dunham, Pauline Crane, Barbara Litchfield, Rhoda Poulter, Winnie Malpas, Marjorie Santler, Joan Payne, headmaster Mr 'Titch' Northern.

Front Row L to R: Peter England, Frankie Herman, Harold Jackson, Gerald Everet, John Turnham, Michael Alcock, George Rowney, Michael Shreeves, Brian Bartram.

classes.

After a couple of years at the Central School, pupils were given another chance to sit for the Bedford Modern Schools. Some of the brighter pupils passed the exam and continued their education there. By the time I got to that stage the school system had changed nationally, and the secondary modern school reared its head. We who had passed the exam for the Harpur Central School felt cheated when in the summer of 1945 our school became a secondary modern school. All children north of the river who had reached the age of eleven and failed the eleven-plus, or who were fourteen but did not wish to leave school, came to our school.

Because of this new education system we lost some of our teachers who went to other schools as heads, but we got the benefit of the best teachers from the town's elementary schools. Among them was the attractive Miss Newbold, from Clapham Road, who was a brilliant French teacher, and Miss Robertson, from Ampthill Road, who brought good music into our lives – we may never have found it without her 'Musical Appreciation Society' on Friday afternoons.

She took us to the BBC Symphony Orchestra's Lunchtime Concerts, which were broadcast from the Corn Exchange, and she arranged for its members to come to our school and demonstrate their instruments, showing us how they came apart and telling us what each part was called. 'Flotsam and Jetsam', the famous singing duo, came and performed for us. We had only ever heard them on the wireless and didn't expect the tall thin man to have the very deep voice and the shorter stouter one, the high voice. We were very privileged to meet such prominent performers and musicians.

On one occasion most of the schools in Bedford were invited to attend the Corn Exchange to hear Moiseiwitsch rehearse Rachmaninoff's Second Piano Concerto. After a few false starts he had the place cleared of children, who he found too distracting. Of course, we said it wasn't anything *we* had done – he just didn't know how to play the piece!

I loved my school and was very happy there. I had always wanted to go to the Central School because it taught lace-making. My great-granny, with whom I had always lived, had been a Bedfordshire lace-maker from Cranfield. She had been taught at the age of three and sold her first yardage of narrow lace at the age of five. Granny didn't teach her own daughters how to make lace; she considered it was slave labour, and any job was better than that. By the time I wanted to learn she was in her late eighties and couldn't see well enough to teach me. At the Central School I was taught to make lace by Mrs Price.

My first-form mistress was Miss Taylor, a wonderful lady who also took the art class. She was well travelled, and kept traditionally dressed dolls – which she had collected from all round the world – in a display cabinet in the art room. One of the stories she told us about her travels was an event which occurred while she and a group of friends were camping in a village in darkest Africa. The tribal chief had insisted on being given a pair of ladies' pink lace-up corsets. He put these on and, with charms and trinkets hanging from the suspenders, proudly paraded around the mud-hut village.

During that first winter at the school it was too wet to use our sports ground at Fairfield in Clapham Road (where

Sainsbury's now stands), so we were taken for walks by the riverside. At eleven and twelve years old we were interested in everything and anything, and one of those things was the huge numbers of 'French letters', or condoms, which floated on the river. We tried counting them, but there were too many. I was worried that they would choke the ducks. 'Don't be daft,' one of the girls replied. 'It's eating all that rubber that keeps the ducks afloat!'

During one of the later winters, when it was too stormy even to go for a walk, Miss Robertson read us a spooky story called 'The Monkey's Paw'. Just when it got to the really frightening part, the classroom window suddenly slammed – and all of us, including the teacher, nearly jumped out of our skins.

The domestic science classes were taken by two very young teachers: Miss Dwyer, who had bright ginger hair, and the glamorous brunette, Miss Hatfield. We were scandalized when we saw them boating on the river with a couple of American Army Air Force officers – our teachers going out with Yanks!

Miss Hatfield taught me domestic science. She was a very pleasant teacher with a great sense of humour, and I enjoyed her classes. What I learned in the laundry lessons put me in good stead for the rest of my life, but cookery wasn't much help. I remember one lesson when we were left on our own in the cookery room to knead bread dough. We were messing about when one of the girls threw her dough up in the air intending to catch it on its way down. To her dismay, it wrapped itself round a steel girder near the ceiling and stayed there. We pelted it with wet dish cloths to try and remove it, but without success.

I enjoyed learning French and tried hard to master it, but I never became fluent. A few holidays in France would have made all the difference, but the war had put a stop to exchange visits. In 1946 Mr and Mrs Wignall arranged a two-week school trip to Holland. Half of us went to Eindhoven and the other half, which I was with, went to Zeeland, where the sluice gates had been opened by the retreating German Army and the land flooded. Going there so soon after the end of the war and seeing what damage sea water did to agricultural land (dead trees with mussels on the branches where leaves should have been) made a great impression on me. Ours was the first school in Bedford to restart school trips abroad.

As well as the usual school subjects, from the age of thirteen we learned shorthand, typing and book-keeping and took Pitmans exams in these skills. The Harpur Central School turned out most of the best secretaries, clerks and office staff in Bedford. We could take the School Certificate if we stayed on, but you had to pass in six subjects to get it. French and Maths, my worst subjects, were compulsory passes and without them I would have come away with nothing – so I chose not to sit for it. My Royal Society of Arts and Pitmans certificates helped to compensate.

At sixth-form level one of our boys (a lovely chap called 'Lucy' Atwell) had blossomed enough to move on to the Bedford Modern School, from where he went to Cambridge – which proves that the eleven-plus exam missed out on some

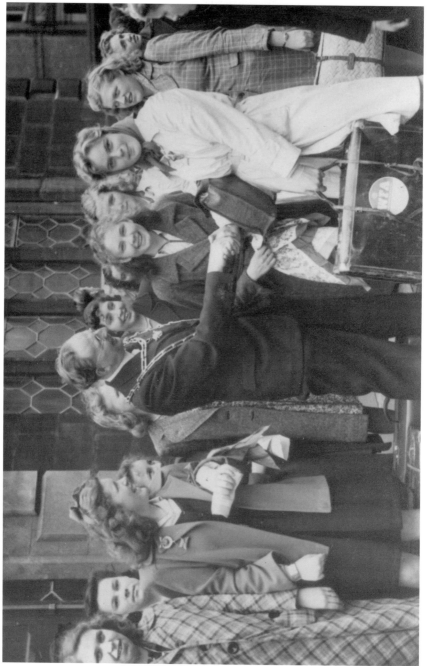

Mayor Canvin and Harpur Central School girls greet Dutch exchange students in 1946.

very promising children!

The Central School had an exceptionally good school canteen. The kitchen also cooked for other schools in the town and transported the food to them in heated containers. Although food was rationed, the dinners were excellent and plentiful. As well as the usual mince, we regularly had the finest veal, roast beef, braised liver and savoury meat roll. For sweet we had rice pudding, of course, but we also had a variety of pastry tarts and custard, wonderful bread and butter pudding, and the most delicious treacle, jam, and chocolate sponge puddings you could wish for.

Bomb damage at the Grosvenor Hotel, Ashburnham Road, 23rd July 1942.

4

WARTIME

With the prospect of war, housewives stocked up with as many household commodities as possible. My mother filled large biscuit tins with various non-perishable foodstuffs including packets of tea. She was devastated when she came to her last biscuit tin and found it did not contain her much-prized packets of tea, but cubes of Foster Clarke's soup powder. She stored tins of shoe and floor polish in the oven of the (never used) kitchen range. One wash day, the copper (which shared the kitchen range chimney) caught fire, melting the polishes, which ran through the oven door and added to the blaze. Luckily it was in daylight and no blackout restrictions were violated.

Eventually all foodstuffs and clothes were rationed, but schoolchildren who were bigger than average were given extra clothing coupons because they needed adult sizes. Every year, at school, we were measured for our height and our feet were measured against two chalk marks on the floor – if your foot went over and not between them, you were eligible for more coupons to buy shoes. I received coupons on both counts.

During the summer of 1939 our ARP Warden, Mr French, called at every house in the street to fit each occupant with a gas mask. I hated having my face covered even when pulling on a jumper, let alone wearing a smelly rubber gas mask, so my friend Cliff and I bunked off to avoid the claustrophobic experience of trying one on. We took a pile of old newspapers to Sammy Nutt's fish-and-chip shop in Hartington Street and exchanged them for a bag of 'scrattlings' (batter bits). We hung around the shop until well after dark, when we thought Mr French would have finished his job. When the siren sounded for the first time, two very frightened children banged on Mr French's front door begging for a gas mask.

The warden also made sure we observed the blackout. After dark, he patrolled the street to see if any of the windows showed a chink of light. I didn't have any problems getting around in the blackout. About the furthest I went on my own in the dark was to Tucker's fish-and-chip shop (the only one that sold crinkle-cut chips) which was next to the prison wall in Tavistock Street. I knew my way perfectly well both by day or night. But my Grandma Hills, who had only recently come to live in Black Tom, was not familiar with the area after dark. She lived with my aunt and uncle in Beaconsfield Street, the next street to ours. One night she left our house (on the corner of Garfield Street and Stanley Street) to make the short journey back. Later, my uncle came round to find out why Grandma had not come home and discovered that she had left about an hour earlier to do the two-minute walk. Mum and Dad went out to help look for her. She was eventually found near Clapham Road School, completely disorientated and in tears. After that, no matter how difficult it was to get batteries, we made sure she had a torch if she went out after dark.

The first evacuees arrived on September 1st in three hospital trains from London. Nearly five hundred patients were taken to the County (South Wing), St Peter's (North Wing), Bromham and Moggerhanger Hospitals. Expectant mothers and mothers with babies and children arrived at Midland Road Station and were marched to the old fairground (where the cattle market was) in Commercial Road. Of Bedford's evacuee children, about five thousand were of school age and most of these arrived on 3rd September, 1939. I remember following the procession of children being taken round the streets of Black Tom looking for billets until it was quite dark.

Clapham Road School took nearly seven hundred children from north London, and the boys of Dame Alice Owen's School, Islington, were allocated to the Bedford Modern School (the Owen Girls' School went to Kettering). In July 1940 another thousand children arrived in Bedford from the south-coast towns of Hastings, St Leonard's, Eastbourne, Seaford and Rye. The Hastings and St Leonard's Central School was integrated with the Harpur Trust Central School, and the Bedford School took a school from Rye, I believe.

Our evacuee, who was a couple of years older than me, belonged to the Kings Warren High School for Girls. They came from Woolwich and Plumstead and attended the Bedford High School. Their dark chocolate-brown uniform was very distinctive and stood out from the other schools, who favoured navy blue or black.

Evacuees assembled at Bedford cattle market for refreshments in September 1939 before being billeted in the town.

It was not the 'done thing' for children to play in the streets on Sundays, and girls from the Kings Warren were not allowed to play in the streets at any time. Instead, they were encouraged to adopt long-forgotten and derelict graves in Foster Hill Cemetery. After church on Sunday mornings, we local children tagged along with them when they tidied up and scrubbed the gravestones of their chosen plots. On the way, in Park Road North, we would stop and peer over the clapboard fence of Mr Ebden's front garden to admire his lily pond. Sitting round the edge were small garden gnomes and a ceramic frog which spouted water from its mouth. There were very few gardens with water features.

One little evacuee boy, Billy, from Islington, was billeted near us. His billet lady was a lovely person, who unfortunately had a speech impediment caused by a facial disfigurement which frightened some children. This boy was used to horses and came to our stables to be with ours. We were both seven years old and played in the cart shed. My mother had hung some pictures – out of the way, because she thought them old-fashioned and didn't like them – on the cart shed walls. To my eyes they were lovely, romantic pictures: a series of Regency scenes of love, courtship and marriage. Billy and I learned to kiss from the picture of 'Love'. We didn't get to courtship or marriage; bombs were not falling on London, so his parents had him home again.

A Jewish family came to live in Stanley Street. The grandmother was orthodox and very devout. On Friday nights, because of her religion, she left the gas stove lit and the water running. When she saw us in the street on Saturday mornings, she would ask one of us to turn the taps off. Some children were afraid to go in; others said they were given tuppence for doing it; but curiosity to see what the inside of the house was like was enough for me. The family was quite well off, but her one room was very basic with only a sink, a gas stove, a table, a couple of chairs and a narrow bed. The curtains were never opened and the low-wattage naked electric light bulb was always on. My mother did some cleaning for her, only once (probably during a religious festival), and touched the table. The table (according to my mother), having been touched by a gentile, was thrown out as being unclean.

The rest of the family were not so strictly orthodox. The two children went to Clapham Road School until they passed the eleven-plus for the Bedford Modern School. Their close relations, who had escaped from Belgium, joined the family too. At Passover they asked me to collect large boxes of unleavened bread from the kosher shop in Bromham Road. I took my bike and brought the boxes back on the crossbar. When I was about twelve I earned pocket money by cleaning their house on Saturday mornings, but I never did the grandmother's room.

At the beginning of the war, soldiers were camped in Bedford Park. On the corner of Park Avenue and Kimbolton Road, opposite the Park Hotel, was their cookhouse, which was just an open-sided corrugated-iron shelter. We were fascinated by the cooking arrangements and amazed to see the food being cooked in dustbins. As long as we didn't make a nuisance of ourselves, our parents had no fear about us wandering amongst the army lorries and talking to the troops.

The soldiers soon moved on and the park returned to normal.

In 1940, after many weeks of being reported as missing, three Black Tom lads – Reg King of Garfield Street, John Elliot of Stanley Street and Tom Anderson of Beaconsfield Street (all aged nineteen) – were found to be safe and well in a German prisoner-of-war camp.

Slit trenches were dug in the Modern School playing field and the gate in the railings at the end of Garfield Street was opened for nearby householders to shelter in the trenches during air raids; but after the first night raid, no one bothered to go into the field again. Later, a circular static water tank, for use by the Fire Brigade, was placed in front of the gate.

A large communal air-raid shelter, with a reinforced concrete roof, was built in Bedford Park where the Robinson Pool now stands. When crowds of people went to use it for the first time, they found three feet of water in it. Although it was regularly pumped out by the Auxiliary Fire Service, it was never really used.

Before he went into the army, one of our neighbours, Mr Rowney, built a concrete shelter for his family in the garden – but that filled with water too, and couldn't be used. Then, like most other people, he fitted out the under-stairs pantry as a safe place for his wife and daughter. My dad didn't kit ours out; his attitude was that if a bomb had your name on it you would get it wherever you were, so when there was an air raid, I would go next door and share Mrs Johnson's pantry. It was company for her as her husband Charlie was in Allen's Fire Brigade and during air raids he went on duty at Allen's Works. My friend Cliff's parents had a Morrison shelter in their living room. The children slept in it every night, which freed up a bedroom for an evacuated mother and child.

Brick air-raid shelters were built in the shrubbery of Clapham Road School and covered with earth. We had regular air-raid practice. As well as carrying a gas mask, we had to pack a snack, such as biscuits, into its case and something to occupy the time should we be forced into a prolonged stay in the shelter. We played cat's cradle, or frayed pieces of cloth by pulling the warp from the weft. The fraying was used by the older girls to stuff soft toys which they made in needlework classes.

On the morning of 23rd July, 1942, we had almost reached the school when a Luftwaffe hit-and-run raider dropped four high-explosive bombs near the old Midland Road railway station. The bombs could be seen falling as the siren sounded. We ran the last few hundred yards and straight into our allotted shelters.

A week later incendiary bombs fell on Albert Street and the surrounding area. My father was up all that night as his mother and sister lived on the corner of Albert Street and Queen Street. My grandmother took refuge in the cellar of Mrs Darlow, who lived opposite and kept an off-licence. Grandma was safe, but my Aunt Mabel sustained a wound when a piece of shrapnel was embedded in her stomach. My great-grandfather's best friend, Arthur Odell, who was in his eighties, lived in Albert Street and was killed when his house was hit by an incendiary bomb. Every householder had been advised to keep a stirrup pump and learn how to use it (my mum and dad had their picture in the Bedford Record giving a

Jim and Gladys Tompkins manning the stirrup pump at a fire fighting demonstration in Garfield Street.

Bomb damage at the Assembly Rooms and Royal County Theatre in July 1942.

demonstration of how to use a stirrup pump), but stirrup pumps were of no use that night.

The morning after, Irene and I took the day off school to view the damage. It was the closest that bombs had got to our houses. Returning to school the following day, we were disciplined for taking the day off. I got away with it because my aunt had been hurt in the raid, but Irene's excuse, that her aunt's house 'was nearly hit by a bomb', was treated with derision.

When a bomb fell on Mr Laxton's house in Kimbolton Road, my mother and I were standing in our front porch. The German plane was flying so low that we could see the men inside it. We were sure we saw the bomb doors open and were really frightened. We threw ourselves flat on the ground. My dad was standing on the street corner and dropped down by the coal-yard fence. Later everyone said he was lucky the bomb didn't drop nearer, because the tons of coal on the other side of the fence would have flattened him.

My friend Margaret's father, Brian Bliss, was in the Fire Service. During the Blitz he was away in London fighting the fires at a terribly dangerous time when fire-storms were feared. He had been a baker before the war, but soon rose to the rank of leading fireman.

We were all urged to save money as part of the war effort. Once a week, at school, we could buy National Savings Stamps. They came in denominations of sixpence (2.5p) or half-a-crown (12.5p). When fifteen shillings' worth (75p) of stamps had been saved, they could be turned into a savings certificate, which matured after five years and earned a little interest. National Savings Stamps became the most popular birthday present – at least for the presenter, if not the recipient. Each street had its own National Savings collector, usually an elderly lady, who called regularly to sell stamps or change them into certificates. These collectors carried what must have been at the time substantial amounts of money, but I never heard of any of them being robbed.

In 1941, when I was nine years old, my friend Cliff and I tried to do 'our bit' by going salvaging on Saturday mornings. We used my Uncle Alf's 'truck', which looked like a coffin on two small pram wheels. It had long wooden handles, which he used to attach to the back of his bike but which made it very unstable to push about. Whilst Cliff and I knocked on doors, his younger sister looked after the truck – which as well as our salvage, contained their two-year-old sister, who sat at one end. If no one kept hold of the handles, the truck tipped up and shot the toddler onto the road.

We chose to collect in the Pemberley Avenue/St Michael's Road area because it was 'posh' and we thought we would get a better class of rubbish than we would nearer home. The most valuable commodity was rabbit skins, valued at sixpence each; but we never got any of those, or any rags, because the regular rag-and-bone men who gave a few pence in exchange got them. We *were* given jam jars, which were profitable: a halfpenny for one-pound, and a penny for two-pound jars.

As well as newspapers, people threw away letters – many written in purple ink on coloured paper. We were quite amazed at this. Whenever our families received a personal letter (always in black ink on white paper) it was kept behind the clock on the mantelpiece for ages, ready to show to friends or relations who called at the house. We were also given quite a number of prayer books and Bibles, but not many ordinary books. Perhaps that was because there were 'book drives' to collect books for the troops and for bombed-out libraries. Books for British prisoners of war were censored, and no books by Jewish authors or H.G. Wells were accepted. Nor were they to include political or controversial subjects, show totalitarian regimes in a bad light or contain instructions for making radios or invisible ink!

We finished our round at lunchtime and took our salvage to Joe Mattin's in Hassett Street. By the side of his terraced house was a wide arch with strong double doors which were closed when business was not being conducted. We joined the queue of trucks on the left-hand side to have our salvage weighed and valued. On the right-hand side were hand carts, the sort that barrow boys and market traders used and that Mr Mattin hired out. From the back of the house the buildings continued to the bottom of the yard, where there were stables, cart sheds and hay lofts, although these were not necessarily used for their original purposes. We were fascinated by the rabbit skins, hung to dry high up on the outside of the lofts. Hundreds of bluebottles buzzed around them.

When we eventually reached the front of the queue, we put our sacks on the large industrial scale for weighing. In the building behind it, Mr Mattin kept valuable metal such as brass, copper, aluminium and lead – we were never given any of that, of course, as people sold it to the proper rag-and-bone men, who resold it at Mattin's. Neat bundles of newspapers, tied with string and taken to the Bedfordshire Times office in Mill Street, would make tuppence (1p) for a three-pound bundle; but ours were stuffed into one of my dad's old chaff sacks. We had no idea what we should be getting for our sacks of paper. We always thought we were being swindled, especially when Mr Mattin put some of our jam jars on one side, saying they were cracked. We didn't see any cracks!

We always made just enough money for the three of us to go to the pictures in the afternoon. After dinner we trawled the cinemas looking for a programme showing two U films. Failing that, we would find a lady in the queue who would take us into an A film. Most children were well practised at saying, 'Would you take us in, Missis?' looking up with beseeching eyes as we proffered our ticket money and added a pathetic 'Please?'.

One Saturday afternoon we couldn't get in at any of the cinemas, so we went to the Royal County Theatre in Midland Road, where we were allowed in. It was almost full with troops who were there to see the show of 'Artistic Poses'. These naked ladies, holding feathered fans, just sat or stood completely still on a revolving stage because, by law, they were not allowed to move. We looked at them with goggle eyes, but would rather have been at the pictures watching Boris Karloff in a good murder!

To help Mrs Churchill's Aid to Russia Fund, I collected bric-a-brac from people in our street and held a jumble sale in our yard. The sum of two pounds was achieved (a week's wage to some people) which was sent off to London and a receipt duly sent back. I wish I had looked after it, but it was lost long ago.

As part of the war effort we collected rosehips, which were used to make rosehip syrup for babies, and conkers – for what purpose we couldn't imagine; we knew that they could not be used for animal feed as they were poisonous. Sixty years later, I found out that they could be used for making explosives! It couldn't have been a very effective explosive, because we were never asked to collect them again.

At the beginning of the war my father went for his medical. When he came home saying he was 'A1', my mother feared he would have to join up. In the end he was not called up because his was a one-man business, and had he gone to war he would have lost his livelihood. He became a fire-watcher instead and took turns with several other householders in our street. They would meet in Mr Street the undertaker's workshop and wait for something to happen. Dad didn't mind sitting among the coffins, but said the clicking of Miss O'Hara's knitting needles got on his wick. As soon as the Home Guard was formed, he joined that. Playing soldiers was more his style; at one time he had been a Territorial with the Royal Horse Artillery.

Dad, Cecil Daniel and 'Waggle' Brace were in the same Home Guard unit and were referred to as 'The Three Musketeers'. My dad was an excellent shot; Dan wasn't much good; but Waggle was absolutely hopeless, and at rifle practice everyone took cover when Waggle was about to shoot. Eventually my dad was given a Sten gun, which he kept unloaded on my mother's dressing table so that he could get at it quickly if it was needed. Its clip of bullets was in the

In the years when our Country

was in mortal danger

JAMES SIDNEY TOMPKINS

who served 4th November 1942 - 31st December 1944

gave generously of his time and

powers to make himself ready

for her defence by force of arms

and with his life if need be.

George R.I.

THE HOME GUARD

Dad's Home Guard Certificate.

Black Tom's Home Guard Unit. Second row from front: tenth from right, Ted King; third from right, Charles (Waggle) Brace, Jim Tompkins and Cecil Daniel at the end. Back row: third from left, John Kidder.

Part of Black Tom's Home Guard Unit.

Top row, left to right: Charles 'Waggle' Brace, Jim Tompkins and Cecil Daniel—'The Three Musketeers'.

top drawer, but no one considered it might be dangerous leaving it about. I was told not to touch it (and that should have been enough), but once or twice I picked it up and handled it.

As part of their training, the Home Guard held night manoeuvres. Because the Three Musketeers each had pieces of ground on the Hoo Farm Allotments and knew the area, even in the dark, like the backs of their hands, they were given the task, on one occasion, of ferreting out the 'enemy' around Bedford's old waterworks. They found a group of them just off the lane, tucked away in a small thicket which was often used as a den by children. The Musketeers threw a couple of thunderflashes into the enemy's cover – the language had to be heard to be believed as they scurried out and were captured! Dad's unit won the day (or rather night), and for a long time they had many a laugh about it.

In the daylight, mock street fighting took place between soldiers and the Home Guard. They ran from one front garden to another, dropping down on their stomachs behind the low walls (where the railings once had been) and shooting blanks at each other. It was great fun. For weeks afterwards the boys played at this, using toy guns or pieces of wood which they pretended were firearms.

Regularly throughout the war, parades took place in Bedford. They started in De Parys Avenue, continued down the High Street, along the Embankment and ended in Russell Park. The Navy marched to encourage us to give money to help buy a battleship, and the Air Force to buy a Spitfire. The Land Army paraded through the town with horses and

The Women's Land Army parading through the town, 1940.

American Troops parading down the High Street during the 'Salute the Soldier Week' in June 1944.

wagons, tractors and all things agricultural. The Home Guard and the Civil Defence added to the swell. When the Americans arrived, their marching bands played fashionable dance music and their modern marching styles delighted the onlookers.

Irene and I were as tall as adults by the time we were ten or eleven years old. Our mothers kept us in ankle socks to show we were still children. What they hadn't realized was that to American servicemen we looked like teenage 'bobby-soxers', and therefore old enough to be dated. So when two Yanks stepped out of E. P. Rose's doorway in the High Street and put their arms around our shoulders, Irene's mother, who was walking a few steps behind us, rushed forward and beat them round their heads with her handbag.

Garfield Street's V-E Day party, May 1945. At end of table and dressed up once again is Gladys Tompkins. Next to her are Cliff Meekins, Barbara Meekins, Cecily Day, Roy Hewitt, Violet Tompkins and Margaret Bliss.

5

AFTER THE WAR

The evening of 7th May, 1945, was warm and sunny, and several of us sat outside on Mrs Bliss's low front-garden wall doing our homework. Everyone was waiting for a radio announcement. The nine o'clock news bulletin told us the war was over and that the following two days were to be national holidays.

As soon as the news was through, everyone (mostly woman and children as the men folk were still at war) congregated in the street. Mrs Daniel, who lived half way down, wheeled her piano close to the front window, started playing popular songs and we all sang along. A Yank appeared from nowhere clutching a bottle of whisky which was passed from one adult to another, each taking a swig from it. Our mothers, who were only in their early thirties but seemed straight-laced middle-aged ladies to us, were drinking from the whisky bottle and singing and dancing in the street! When it got dark, bonfires were lit, often in the most inappropriate places, and we went down to the embankment to see the coloured lights, which hadn't been on since before the war. They stretched out among the trees along the river bank and over the Town Bridge.

The following day a hastily-prepared street party was held. From under the counter – or from housewives' precious store cupboards – jellies, blancmanges and other rarely-seen foodstuffs were set out on the tables. When the tea was over, two Yanks arrived looking for the American Red Cross in Bromham Road (which had been Langley's car showrooms). My friend Margaret and I volunteered to take them there, and as we walked down the street, one put his arm round me. Precociously I told him, 'I'm just an overgrown schoolgirl!' To which he replied, 'That's all right. I'm just an overgrown schoolboy, just shipped out!' Before we reached the bottom of the street, Mrs Hewitt came and dragged us back. Had we lost our last chance to get a Yank, we wondered?

Victory Parades were organised, and again the Americans marched in their distinctive style to their modern music. The American servicemen seemed to leave the Bedford area very quickly when the war ended, but Cardington Camp was inundated with handsome, young, blond Dutch airmen. Again we cursed our luck for being too young to date them. We were growing up, but it seemed that all the fun and excitement was passing us by.

In August, a few days after the atomic bombs were dropped on Japan, the war in the Far East ended. Street parties were held for V-J Day and again parades took place, but it didn't have the impact on us that V-E Day had done.

The public could now start thinking about holidays by the sea again. The Hewitt family took me with them when they went to Bournemouth for a week. We went in their car, and to save petrol (which was still on ration) we had to get out and push it up the steepest hills. The seaside town was crowded with American servicemen, and Glen-Miller-style music came belting out of the dancehall. It was a pleasure in the evenings to sit in the public gardens and listen to it.

Our own servicemen returned from the war. Their houses were decorated with flags and banners to welcome the heroes home and the whole street turned out to cheer them. An even greater effort was made for returning prisoners of war, especially those from the Far East who had suffered so badly under the Japanese. When our neighbour Mr Rowney (who had built the air-raid shelter in his garden) returned, he didn't know what to do with all that concrete. Being a very artistic man, he successfully turned the whole area into a model village, complete with a miniature windmill and watermill. When each serviceman was demobilized, he was issued with a 'demob' suit, a hat and shoes. One of Dad's customers, who was used to bespoke tailoring, sold his navy-blue, pinstriped demob suit to my dad, which served him admirably for many years.

Although during the war years our food had been rationed, all the available food had been for our own country's consumption. Following the end of the war, we had to help feed the rest of Europe. These were the austerity years. Bread was rationed for the first time, and there were bread queues. On Saturday mornings my mother used to send me as far afield as St John's Street to buy stale cakes from Hester's Bakery. These were not the delicate patisserie that we can buy from today's supermarket bakeries, but real stomach-fillers.

Garfield Street's V-E Day party, May 1945.

Clearing the Albert Street bomb site ready for the V-E Day party.

Author (left) with friend in Mr Rowney's back-garden model village.

Clothes and dress materials were still rationed, but things started getting better with a greater choice in dress fabrics. We sometimes took the train to Northampton, where we could buy dress material at the market without giving up clothing coupons. During my last year at school, I would cut out a dress or skirt in my needlework class, bring it home, make it up on my ancient treadle sewing-machine, take it back the following week to get it marked and then cut another one out. No clothing coupons changed hands. This set me up with clothes to start work. The teacher must have realized what I was doing, but after years of school uniform dresses (made from green material that had originally been issued to the school for making into canteen tablecloths) she knew that we needed clothes suitable for work.

The winter of 1946–47 was very hard, with exceptionally heavy falls of snow. This gave us an extra-long season to go tobogganing on the slopes of Franklin's Fields in Clapham Road. Also using the slopes with their home-made sledges were German prisoners of war, whose camp was nearby. It was our first encounter with the 'enemy'. Some were only eighteen years of age and had already been POW's for over two years. On the whole they seemed to be pleasant young men, but fraternising was forbidden. In the months that followed, they were able to mix freely with the public and sold handmade wooden toys and children's rope sandals to appreciative parents.

Although coal had been rationed all through the war, in 1947 there was hardly any to be had. Because he couldn't supply them, my father suffered personal abuse from some of

his customers. They barged into our house to see if we had a
fire ourselves, even though we had two grandmothers, one in
her eighties and the other in her nineties, living with us.
Someone even came in and lifted the cloth to see if we had
any coal hidden under the table. My dad had never been heard
to swear before, but this tipped him over the edge.

The truth is that we never *ever* had a decent fire – except
on Christmas and Boxing days – and our fire was always
made from the sweepings off the coal cart. A more
uncomfortable house you couldn't imagine: the back door was
always wide open for customers, and the fire banked down
with slack. Even if you were lucky enough to own an electric
fire, you couldn't always use it because at that time we were
also plagued with power cuts. Some people went to the
cinema to keep warm, but the programme would be
suspended when the electricity was cut.

After the snow came the thaw. The river flooded and some
of the town was under water – including the Harpur Central
School, which gave me time off.

The summer that followed was glorious. With Double
British Summer Time we had daylight from dawn till eleven
at night, and most of it was continuous sunshine. With two or
three friends, I spent a lot of time on Dad's smallholding plot,
lying in the long grass, listening to music from a portable
gramophone.

In the autumn, I went old-time dancing with my mother at
St Martin's Hall. Later, I went to Clapham Road Youth Club,
run by Maurice Hullat, where we played table tennis and
learned ballroom dancing before chancing the Corn Exchange

or the Drill Hall. At the Crofton Rooms, which had a sprung floor, we learned square dancing as we went along. The ballroom was packed with dancers do-si-doing and allemanding in all the wrong directions. It was hilarious, and we laughed till the tears ran down our faces.

Although the war was over, there were still servicemen at the Corn Exchange dances. Some of them were in bright-blue uniforms with red ties and came from Grange Camp at Kempston, which was the 101 Convalescent Depot. These soldiers smelled so strongly of iodine that unless they were extremely good looking we didn't like to dance with them.

The Birch Bus ran every hour, almost round the clock, to and from London. It enabled people to go dancing at Cardington and Henlow Camps (my dad never let me go there) and to get to London to see the shows. In 1951 when the Festival of Britain took place at London's South Bank and the Pleasure Gardens at Battersea Park, we were able to get there, cheaply and often, on the Birch Bus.

Bedford was changing, and in the 1950s and 1960s many of the older houses were pulled down and tall blocks of flats built to replace them. One morning in the early 1950s, my dad, with his horse and cart, was on his way to the station yard to pick up a delivery of coal. A new block of flats on the corner of Woburn Road and Ashburnham Road was being built. Just as my dad was going past, the builders threw something heavy into an empty lorry, which made a sudden and very loud bang. The horse took fright and bolted towards the old station yard. As it galloped down Ashburnham Road, the unladen trolley was pulled along as if it were made of

The Queen Street flats being built, viewed from the top end of Garfield Street.

balsa wood. It swung from one side of the road to the other, crashing into cars parked at the roadside. The horse came to a standstill at the coal yard. It was unharmed and little damage was done to the cart, but my dad was staggered by the size of the claims made by the car owners against his insurance company. Until then he had not learned to drive because he thought the motor would never take the place of the horse, but now he realized he was wrong. Later, my husband gave him driving lessons, although by then Dad felt he was getting too old to learn. It was when they were practising on the (thought to be) disused Podington airfield and an aircraft suddenly came in to land, that Dad gave up the effort for good!

In 1947 I left school and the following week started work in the front office at Meltis (the chocolate and confectionery manufacturer) as a junior shorthand typist. At school I had used a brand-new Remington typewriter which had come straight from America, but at work I was given a battered old Royal. I was never given any shorthand dictation. To fill our time during the day, the Comptometer operator showed me how to do fashion drawing. Then, at five o'clock, all the day's typing would suddenly come down to me and I was expected to have it done in time to catch the five-thirty post – I just couldn't cope. I realized I didn't like office work and after only six months I left.

Next, I took a job at Bennett's Clothing Factory in Castle Lane making school uniforms, which I enjoyed. It was more relaxed than an office, and while we worked we sang our way through the day. I made school blouses and dresses, except for doing the buttonholes and putting on the buttons. The skills I learned there were invaluable.

After several years I left Bennett's and came back to the Black Tom to work at Hallwin's Proper Pride Lingerie in Park Road East. Working in a production team and making only parts of petticoats, rather than whole garments, gave me no satisfaction. One day, when I had been there for less than a year, I decided not to go back after lunch and went instead to the 'War Ag' (War Agricultural Committee) in Ashburnham Road to look for a new job. What made me go there, rather than to the employment exchange, I shall never know; but it was a decision that was to change the whole course of my life. They had just been told of a vacancy at Unilever. I went for the interview and was lucky enough to land a good job at the Colworth food laboratory in Sharnbrook. I was to work there, full- and part-time, for thirty years, and it was there that I met my husband, who was working in another section.

We married in 1954 at my parish church of St Martin's, near my first school in Clapham Road, and moved into our first home – a farmhouse at Colworth. We later moved to a cottage in Wymington, and lastly to our house on the rural border between Bedfordshire and Northamptonshire, where we still live today; but the Black Tom area of my childhood, with all its characters and memories, will always be my spiritual home – my 'neck of the woods'.

Gladys, Violet, Jill Day and Jim Tompkins after work.

The author on her father's cart in 1938 (Mrs Knowles' shop in background).

The horse and cart in Garfield Street.

Day's work done: my father taking off the horse's harness.

A very early photo of Cecil Daniel and his lorry in Gladstone Street.

Later picture of Cecil Daniel's lorries in his yard.

Roy Hewitt with the car we pushed up the hills on holiday.

The shops in Russell Street (now part of Queen Street). The shop on the far left was Whittemore's; next was Irving's newsagents; then Garwood's Butcher's shop. The cleared space near the tree was where the Consumers Tea Company stood.

Corner of Park Road West and house in Little Garfield Street before demolition.

Park Road East seen from Park Road West, after demolition of the above houses.

The corner of Russell Street & Little Garfield Street. These houses stood where the north-east corner of Boswell Court is today.

Young's Off-Licence on the corner of Canning Street & Russell Street (now the north-east corner of Boswell Court).

Albert Street V-E Day party from the Queen Street end.

Albert Street V-E Day party from the Wellington Street end.

Albert Street V-E Day party.

The author, aged 13, on holiday in Bournemouth with the Hewitt family in 1945.